TERRY FATOR
WHO'S THE DUMMY NOW?

First published in Australia in 2008 by
New Holland Publishers (Australia) Pty Ltd
Sydney • Auckland • London • Cape Town
Unit 1/66 Gibbes Street Chatswood Australia
218 Lake Road Northcoate Auckland New Zealand
New Edgeware Road London W2 2EA United Kingdom
80 McKenzie Street Cape Town 8001 South Africa

www.newholland.com.au
www.youngreed.com.au

A record of this book is held at the National Library of Australia

ISBN 9781741107289

Publishers: Fiona Schultz and Linda Williams
Publishing Manager: Lliane Clarke
Project Editor: Christine Chua
Cover Design: Hayley Norman
Production Manager: Linda Bottari
Printed in the United States of America

TERRY FATOR
WHO'S THE DUMMY NOW?

NEW
HOLLAND

In memoriam

Our cat, Lamu, who was our joy
for seventeen years before finally leaving us
for kitty heaven.

I wish to acknowledge all my friends—
Darrell and Sissy Johnson, and
Wayne and Sally Kirkham especially—
and family
—Debi, Jep, Pam, Alyssa and Shirley chiefly—
who believed in me over the years,
and above all,
my wife Melinda.

Contents

Chapter 1
The Million-Dollar Voice

I stood in front of the cameras on live television, palms sweating, intensely uncomfortable under the hot lights, waiting to hear the results. So far I had survived two anxious rounds, somehow keeping myself from passing out as the tension mounted more each time, wondering along with all of America what the end result would be.

The evening had been truly historic from my perspective. I had fulfilled a dream of mine since I was very young; that of performing live with Kermit the Frog, but it had been so much more than just singing with Kermit. The producers of *America's Got Talent* had pulled out all the stops for my final performance on the show, and had literally rebuilt the entire stage to accommodate not only Kermit (for whom they had created an entire forest on the stage), but had also taken out the judges' chairs and substituted them with seating for the replacement Muppet judges: Animal, the Swedish Chef and Beaker, all of whom any Muppet fan will recognize instantly.

The performance with Kermit had been surreal at best. I kept thinking how it simply must be a dream. *I can't be actually standing next to Kermit, singing a duet with him through my puppet*, *Johnny Vegas*, who was doing a very good (if I do say so myself) impression of James Taylor's version of Carole King's classic *You've Got A Friend*. I was so overwhelmed I even stepped on one of Kermit's lines! (Thankfully the mistake was left in the show, reminding me forever of how completely blown away I was by that moment.)

Once we finished the song, Animal began chanting 'Terry! Terry! Terry!' Surely none of this can really be happening. Soon I will find myself in my bed at home, waking up to a normal day, happy to have had such a pleasant vision.

But it *was* happening, and I was living through it all. The Muppet judges gave me high marks in their own unusual ways, and then another surprise: I had a special message from someone sending me her love all the way from London via satellite. It was Miss Piggy, offering me a personal message, actually saying *my* name on national television. OK, now I *know* this isn't real. There is no way Miss Piggy knows who the heck I am.

But once again I didn't wake up. It really happened just as I described it, and I was here now, in the final moments of the television show *America's Got Talent Season 2*, waiting to find out if I would take second place—or the whole enchilada.

We had spent the entire week rehearsing a group number with the top ten contestants. The number went perfectly, and the other top contestants had been called up twice already, leaving only myself and Cas Haley, a fantastic singer who sang with such feeling and soul I got chills every time I heard him.

My competition in this final show had been formidable: Julienne Irwin, a lovely young lady who had never sung in public, had performed one of the nicest versions of *Somewhere*

Over The Rainbow I had ever heard, the act culminating with her floating down to the stage on a crescent moon, leaving the audience awestruck.

Butterscotch, a beautiful woman who can beat box (create the sounds of percussion through the use of her voice and lips), sing and play piano at the same time, had also wowed the studio audience and America with a stunning performance.

Cas had done his usual magic by singing a Stevie Wonder song with his band, leaving me with goose bumps galore as always.

I had spent the week before agonizing about how I would top the performances that had taken me into this spot in the first place. Week after week I had been under the gun to make each performance better than the last, and had gone to the well of routines I had perfected during the years of entertaining live all over the country, but I had no idea what I would do for my finale.

Luckily three important people in my life—my wife, my sister, and my mother-in-law—knew exactly what I should do, and I am so glad I listened to them. They had been pressuring me during the entire run of the show to do my Roy Orbison impression, something that I had done for years. The only trouble was that I had never done the voice without moving my lips, and I had no idea which puppet would be right to sing it.

Well, a professional shines when the pressure is on, so I submitted the song *Crying* by Roy Orbison to the producers of *America's Got Talent* and waited to hear back from them. Their response? 'Can you actually do an impression of Roy Orbison? Why didn't you tell us before?'

'Yeah, sure!' I exclaimed, not mentioning that I had no idea if I could do it ventriloquially. The producer let me know the next day that the song had been cleared. I could do it. Now down to the hard work, learning to sing it through a puppet. But first I had to decide *which* puppet!

I was lying in bed late that night when an idea struck me like a lightning bolt. *Winston* would sing it! Of course it had to be Winston the Impersonating Turtle. Winston had come out and done his impression of Kermit the Frog while I did my impression of Louis Armstrong and we had sung *What A Wonderful World*, and together had struck a chord with America. I was getting emails daily from people all over the country about how much they loved Winston and how they would YouTube our version of *What A Wonderful World*, and that it would make them feel good even on a bad day.

But I think the next idea was the clincher: not only would Winston sing the song, but I would dress him in a little black wig and sunglasses for the performance. In spite of the late hour I immediately called my wife, Melinda, and told her, 'Honey, I think I just came up with a million-dollar idea!' I explained my inspiration, and she said, 'I think you may be right.'

The next day I told my producer Elyse Foley what I had shared with Melinda the night before (each of us had been assigned a producer to help us throughout the show). Elyse's response? Exactly the same as Melinda's! Hopefully I was on to something, but now came the arduous task of teaching Winston how to sing like Roy Orbison.

I began to work ten hours a day, listening to *Crying* a hundred times daily, learning every nuance of Roy Orbison's voice, and working out how to recreate the sounds through barely opened lips. I also had to choreograph Winston's every movement, making each one count, eliciting the proper emotion every second we were on stage.

The night finally arrived, and Winston and I performed the song before the live studio audience, the judges, and all of America through their television sets.

The judges were absolutely blown away, and English journalist Piers Morgan, the 'mean' Simon Cowell-type of the group actually gave me a standing ovation, saying that I would be 'Crying all the way to the bank, because I think you've just won a million dollars'. I was delirious! But the question loomed: Would America agree with Piers? How would America vote? The only thing left was to wait out the long week.

The finale was live, so the pressure was on. We did pre-tape some of the more difficult stuff, like my duet with Kermit and the Muppet judges' responses. Performing with the Muppets was the most fun I've ever had. The Muppet performers were always improvising and never did a take the same way, but it was always funny. They are simply geniuses and I was so honoured to have the opportunity to work with them. I have never laughed as much as I did that night, and it is something I will never forget.

Some of the other duets with the top four were also pre-taped, but the bulk of the show would be broadcast live for all of America to see. It opened with the song *Celebration* performed by the last ten contestants, ending with the remaining four of us center stage.

Slowly the night crept toward the ending. One routine after another finished, then they called all four of us to the stage to nervously await our fate.

Julienne was the first to go, and she handled it like a real pro in spite of the fact that she was so new to all of this. As we left the stage I hugged her tightly and told her that she would have a fabulous career no matter what happened tonight.

More performances and more waiting, then the top three were called to the stage to continue the eliminations.

After several more panic-inducing moments, Butterscotch was announced as the next to leave. I had made it to the top two! Only one elimination round left!

The show continued to roll with more time-filling entertainment, but I don't remember much of it. I was overwhelmed by the idea that only one elimination round was left and I was to be a part of it!

Finally the moment I had worked my whole life for arrived. Cas Haley and I were called to the stage to find out our fate.

As I stood in front of America, my heart began to pound in a way I had never thought possible. I could feel it pulsing, pounding on my rib cage relentlessly, threatening to break through my chest at any moment. I felt a little dizzy and swept up in the moment. I was really here, in front of millions of people, waiting with all of them to find out if I had done what I had never dreamed possible, being named the best new act in America, and walking away with a million dollars!

As the tension built I wondered how much longer my heart could stand this. Host Jerry Springer was stalling, making each moment last as long as he could, building the tension masterfully. I found out later that the teleprompter had gone out and he'd to ad lib. Had he not told me afterward what had happened I would have never known, since he handled the situation like a pro.

Suddenly I looked out at the crowd. I saw my family, hands clenched tightly, looking almost as nervous as I felt.

Then I saw my wonderful wife, Melinda. Our eyes locked, and I was instantly filled with a strange calm. Yes this was my dream, but whatever the outcome, she would still be there as she had been for the past seventeen years, believing in me, encouraging me to dream, and knowing that one day those dreams would come true.

I had no idea the camera was on me as I mouthed the words 'I love you' to Melinda. I didn't care one way or the other. All I cared about at that moment was her. She had meant so much to me for the better part of my life, and without her none of this could have been possible, and I just wanted her to know that right then.

But once again reality came rushing back like a burst dam, and I realized that the moment of truth was very near.

After much more stalling, Jerry Springer finally said the words all of us had been waiting to hear: 'America has decided,' he said. 'The winner *of America's Got Talent*, the winner of the title 'Best New Act in America', and the winner of ONE MILLION DOLLARS is...' Can fifteen seconds feel like ten minutes? Jerry Springer paused after those words for fifteen seconds, during which my mind raced with the thoughts and feelings I had been through over these past few months. Countless hopes and dreams were riding on the next two words. Would Jerry say 'Cas Haley' or my name? Finally, he said it: 'Terry Fator!'

I have been asked how I felt at that moment. I think the words of Gene Wilder as *Willy Wonka* in the original '70s version of the film say it perfectly: 'You know what happened to the little boy who suddenly got everything he always wanted? He lived happily ever after!'

I was instantly swept into a dream. I know that Winston sang 'Crying' again, but I don't remember much of it. Afterward the stage was flooded with people; some of the other contestants of the show came out and hugged me, congratulating me, but the only ones I wanted to see were my family.

The first was Melinda. She came on stage in tears and said, 'You did it! Oh, Baby, you did it!'

I grabbed her and kissed her, saying, 'This is really happening, isn't it?'

She laughed and kissed me again.

I held her tightly and said to her, 'Now I can give you the life you have always dreamed of.'

She said back, 'You've already given me the life I've always dreamed of.'

To which I replied, 'Ok then, I can give you the life *I've* always dreamed of giving *you*!'

As all this was happening, Jerry Springer was helping my sister onto the stage. Debi had been diagnosed with rheumatoid arthritis when she was eighteen and had suffered for many years and could barely walk, so she needed help getting to me through the crowd.

Throughout the process of the show I had always told Debi that if I won I would pay to get a very expensive treatment for her disease that none of us had been able to afford. It had seemed like a pipedream every time I had promised it, but as she came onstage and hugged me, I whispered to her, 'Call your doctor and arrange to get the treatment. We're going to get you feeling better.' She burst into a new wave of tears, overwhelmed by happiness, as we all were.

Quickly, I was whisked away to a sea of cameras, doing interview after interview with the top entertainment shows in the world: *Entertainment Tonight, Access Hollywood, Inside Edition, TV Guide Channel*, and many more.

It all seems like a blur now, but after dinner with my friends and family, Melinda and I finally found ourselves in our hotel room, away from the sights and sounds of the world, lying quietly in the darkness, and for the next hour or so one of us would say, 'We just won a million dollars!'

and we would burst into fits of giggling until I would say, 'Quiet, I have to get up at three and do *The Today Show*!' Then I would add ecstatically, 'I'm doing *The Today Show*!' and we would burst into more fits of laughter. This went on for hours until we finally settled into silence, and since I couldn't sleep, my mind swirled with the experiences of my life that had led me here, as a new millionaire about to embark on a whole new chapter of my life and career, a chapter that I had dreamed of and worked for since I was a very small child.

I had finally crossed the chasm that had seemed so impossible to bridge, but my persistence and tenacity, along with the encouragement of my friends and family, wouldn't allow me to give up.

My alert brain drifted to my childhood as I relived the defining moments of my life, as clearly as though they had just happened, although some of these memories were almost forty years old. I was delirious with the thought that those moments had led me here, now, to this room, calm after the culmination of every dream I had dreamt since I was ten had come true on this very night.

I'll have to warn you now that I have ADD (attention deficit disorder), and tend to jump from one topic to another. My goal for this book is to let you inside my head, and if you think you can handle it, read on, my friend I just thought I'd warn you.

Now, let's see, where to begin...

Chapter 2
Beginnings

All stories have a beginning, and mine began in the early morning hours of June 10, 1965 in Dallas, Texas.

I was the second child of my parents, Jephtha and Marie Fator, born a year and a half after my brother Jephtha Fator Jr, whom we all used to call Jeppie.

Much of this chapter will have to be anecdotal because I have very little memory of the first years of my life, but I have a good idea of the type of child I was from the stories my mother and brother tell me.

I began to speak at a very young age; at nine months old I was able to repeat certain words that adults would say to me. I know it sounds crazy, but I suppose it was just the natural gift for impressions that allowed me to repeat words spoken. At just one year old I could repeat pretty much any word, and I became quite popular among the adults who associated with my parents and who would say words like 'helicopter' and 'hippopotamus' and I could repeat it to them eagerly.

Most of my life I have been in the spotlight and enjoyed it. I was a very headstrong, stubborn kid, and my mother tells me that when I was two, she or my father would tell me not to touch something and I would defiantly reach my hand out and touch it. My parents would smack my hand, and I would stubbornly reach out and touch it again.

This battle of wills would continue until my hand was beet-red, and my lips would be quivering from the discomfort of my hand hurting, yet I wouldn't give up. I would continue to defy my parents' orders and reach out and touch the object.

It was a different time, when many parents believed that children should obey rules, and thankfully my parents never let me win these battles of wills. I believe it was their persistence to teach me that rules must be obeyed that taught me self-control. I hesitate to think what I may have become if I had been left to my own devices and whims, since I tend to gravitate to being undisciplined and idle—but I am able to take control of those desires and work very hard; I believe this is because my parents simply demanded I control myself when the need arose.

I always loved the spotlight, never shying away from attention. My mother tells me a story about when I was three and my Sunday school class was to recite John 3:16 in Spanish before the congregation.

Before we went on, my mother says, my father told me to speak loudly and clearly so everyone could hear. We all started, but I was so much louder than the other children that they trailed off and I was left to recite the verse alone, shouting clearly as instructed. After I was finished the teacher said, 'Thank you, Terry. That was lovely. Now let's have the whole class recite it together.'

We started up again and ended with the exact same result, with me reciting the verse even louder than before, so I could be heard above the laughter of the adults in the audience.

I worshiped my older brother and followed him around everywhere like his shadow, and I remember a joyous day when I was three that my father announced we were going to the hospital to pick up a baby sister. I recall the excitement of realizing that I would have a baby sister.

My tiny overactive brain pictured a baby factory where my new little sister was being manufactured, and I thought it was such a coincidence that my mother happened to be sick in the hospital at the very same time my new sister was ready to be picked up.

On the way to the hospital I asked what our new sister's name was and my dad said she didn't have a name yet. I clearly remember saying 'Can we name her Froggy?' I have no idea why I wanted to name her Froggy. Perhaps I sensed that one day I would be a celebrity and Froggy would seem normal compared to the goofy names many celebrities gave their children, but thankfully my parents did not share this premonition, and sanity prevailed. They named my sister Deborah. We call her Debi. We used to spell it 'Debbie', but one day when she was five she announced to the family that she wanted to spell her name Debi from now on and it stuck, so Debi it is to this very day.

I always felt a special bond with her. I was a tiny waif of a kid, much smaller than children of my age, so Debi quickly outpaced me growth-wise and was taller and bigger than I was by the time she was five and I was eight. I never felt like her protector, but I always took care of her as well as I could, despite my small stature. She tells me that every day I would walk her to school, carry her books and give her a kiss on the cheek as I dropped her off at her classroom. I would also meet her after school and walk her home.

One of my first clear memories is when I was three years old. I was standing on a table at my church, singing a song in front of a large group of adults. They were all clapping and laughing, and I remember thinking that I really liked this feeling, wanting it as often as possible.

I was in every single church and school play or presentation and it didn't take long for my teachers to figure out that I was incredibly anxious to perform, so I usually got the lead in any show I tried out for.

At six I found a stack of old LPs in my dad's closet and fished out a Bill Cosby record and a José Jiménez album. I had a little child's record player and I began to play those two records constantly. I have no idea why I loved them so much, since I was too young to understand most of the jokes and stories they told, but for some reason I just loved them.

In a few days I had pretty much memorized both albums word-for-word and was able to recite any of the routines, using the same inflections as Bill Cosby and José Jiménez, much to the delight of my parents and their friends. José Jiménez was a comedian who would do his comedy using a Spanish accent and I remember the adults around howling with laughter every time I would start off one of his routines with those immortal words: 'My name José Jiménez!' and then continuing on until the routine was concluded.

I had no idea I was doing impressions because I was too young to know what the heck an impressionist was; all I knew was that I enjoyed doing the voices and I got big laughs by doing them.

My favorite Bill Cosby skit was called 'Little Tiny Hairs', which was about a sports star selling a new brand of razor and he would, in a dull, thick, goofy voice, say, 'Always use… a razor… on my face to shave…' long pause for comedy effect… 'It!' to howls of laughter from my parents and their friends.

I probably learned my comic timing from these episodes of reciting these comedy routines for my parents and anyone who would listen. I learned that when a pause was too short or too long it could affect the amount of laughter I elicited from the audience. I would notice the subtleties of when a particular voice would get the best laugh at just the right moment, and I would tailor each routine to get the most amount of laughter I could.

I haven't spoken much of my parents yet because for the first few years of my life we had what seemed to me a very ordinary family life. We had a mom, a dad, and three children, pretty much the typical family of the late '60s.

I loved to watch TV, and I especially loved colorful shows like *Batman* and *Laugh In*. I was far too young to see the satire of Adam West's *Batman*. All I knew was that he would get himself into terrible jams, thanks to the evil super-villains, and I could hardly wait to find out how he would get out of them. My brother Jep was roughly twice my size so he always got to be Batman as our imaginations took us deep into the heart of Gotham City, routing out any and every speck of evil we could find. I was his faithful sidekick, Robin, and happily so.

My mother tells me that when I was three she came into the kitchen and found that I had tied a towel around my neck as a cape and climbed up onto the counter and was going to jump off in my pursuit to rid the house of all crime.

My imagination had no bounds and I always built up everything around me to be far more amazing and interesting than reality can possible be. I am the king of exaggeration and my wife still laughs at how, when I tell her anything regarding numbers, she can pretty much divide it by ten to get the actual number. I'll say, 'There were a hundred thousand people there!' to which she'll reply, 'So about ten thousand showed up, huh?' with a twinkle in her eye. I don't mean to be dishonest; this is how I see the world.

A good example of this occurred when I was eight. I had saved my money for weeks to buy something I had seen in an ad in a comic book. 'Remote-Controlled Ghost!', the ad screamed. 'YOU Control It! Amaze and Scare Your Friends! It Really Flies!!!'

I finally had enough money to send away for it and I waited as patiently as a child could while my brain created all of the possibilities open to me with my very own remote-controlled ghost. I saw myself holding a remote, bringing it to school and having it fly around the halls, around the corners. I would be the most popular kid in school with my ghost! If a bully tried to pick on someone, here comes Terry to the rescue as his ghost flies up and scares the bully away.

I could hardly wait until it arrived. These were the days before we could order something online and have it two days later. The ad said, 'Allow six to eight weeks for delivery' and it meant it. I spent the whole six to eight weeks creating scenarios in which my new ghost and I would take part. Then it arrived. I remember seeing the package and saying to myself, *Gosh, the package is awfully small. I wonder how they got the ghost inside?*

It turned out it was a plastic sheet about two feet by two foot, a string and a balloon. The instructions said to blow the balloon up, wrap it in the sheet to create a head, draw a face on it and string it between two trees, pulling it from one to another to make it 'fly'.

As disappointed as I was, it did nothing to dampen my excitement of the Sea-Monkeys that would arrive in six to eight weeks!

The picture on that ad showed a little family of human-like sea creatures supping in front of their castle.

'You can even train them!' the ad screamed.

Once again I imagined a thousand scenarios with my new pets. I would teach them to bow when my friends came over and would always take good care of my new little family. I would hold races and have special days for them to play. I had even devised a way I could give them vacations from their bowl, provided they were good and would return without argument.

Then they arrived. I had to mix the solution and put the eggs in so they could hatch, then wait another twenty-four hours before my new pals would be part of my life. They turned out to be little brown multi-legged things that swam aimlessly around in a murky solution. I tried to put on the best face I could and actually named a few of them, but they all got black spots and died soon after.

Time after time I experienced this same kind of disappointment, but I never got cynical; I never stopped dreaming.

If all this seems strange to you, don't forget that I have made a career of making people think that puppets are alive. There is no doubt in my mind that it is my limitless imagination that made me ever think I could do that.

In spite of how my expectations always far exceeded what reality could provide, I never felt too shattered and would simply move from one dream to another, blithely unaware of the simple facts that always crept up and told me that dreaming was silly, and that I should wake up and accept reality.

As I grew ever older in my quest to find something magical about life, I slowly began to learn that all of the things I thought truly amazing were, in fact, just make-believe. Santa Claus, the Easter Bunny, and more, fell by the wayside as creations of fantasy.

I'll never forget the day my mother took me and Jep to see Winnie the Pooh live and in person. I was so disappointed to find out that it was just some guy in a costume and not the real cartoon character. A couple of years later, we went to see *Sesame Street* live on stage and I argued with a couple of teenagers all the way home, convinced that Big Bird was not a puppet because I had seen him live on stage. I never wanted to face the facts that the icons of our childhood were created for children only and had never been reality, but were designed for us to shed as we grew into adulthood.

I always resisted these facts and in spite of what I knew to be true I still convinced myself that they were real. I don't want you to think that I was delusional. This couldn't be further from the truth. I saw things as they really were; I just wanted my life to be filled with wonder, so I held onto the magic because it made life more fun.

I was also never afraid to put my feelings out there to be accepted or rejected. When I was eight I developed a hopeless crush on my teacher, Lindy Timberlake. Never one to hide my feelings, I wrote her an impassioned letter, telling her how much I loved her. Thankfully she had the foresight to give the letter to my mom, who later put it in a photo album, giving it to me when I got married. I still laugh when I read that letter. I can't believe I had the guts to do that!

I never felt crushed to learn that Santa was more of an idea than a fact; I just liked the *idea* that he was there, and pretended that he was. I still like to pretend and even though I am in my forties, Santa has visited my house every single year of my life since I chose to make it so.

I never thought of Kermit the Frog as a puppet who had a human being below him making him come alive. I thought of him as Kermit the Frog, plain and simple. Even when I got the call from Kermit during *America's Got Talent* I laughed afterward about the fact that in my mind I was imagining Kermit on the phone speaking with me. I have had a lot of training with pretending and it served me well in my teenage years as I will explain later.

When I was eight my father came home from work and performed a little close-up magic trick he found at a magic store that happened to be near where he worked. I was hooked. Even though once again it was only pretend magic, it made life seem more than just mundane—so I decided I wanted to be a magician.

Life as a kid in those days was full of outdoor adventures. My brother and I rode our bikes to every section of our town, exploring every body of water within a ten-mile radius in the hope that it may garner us a few fish for dinner.

We would come home after a particularly hard day's fishing on a long, hot summer afternoon, carrying a string of thirty or forty tiny bream and perch we had caught. They were no larger than the minnows we used for bait, but we had caught each and every one of them, and by gum, we would eat them. My mother would clean and fry the fish, and we ate them with the same satisfaction that early man must have had looking at his family as they enjoyed the spoils of his day's hunt.

But at night, when our outdoor adventures had come to an end, I would dream of the day I was a world-famous magician just like Houdini. I read everything I could about him and decided that I would be like him, touring everywhere and amazing everyone with my incredible abilities.

I spent every moment of my evenings from then on, for the next year and a half, scouring magic catalogues from Jefferies Magicland (our local magic store), dreaming of owning each and every illusion in the book. I would write routines for tricks I didn't even have and would spend hours practicing the ones I did. I became quite good at sleight-of-hand magic and was able to cut a deck of cards with one hand, and could fan out a deck perfectly every time. I worked on coin tricks and card tricks, the linking rings and the ball-and-cup routines. I could multiply little yellow sponge rabbits magically and conjure billiard balls from thin air.

My parents bought me Mark Wilson's *Complete Course of Magic* and I studied it faithfully every night, learning more and more about how to amaze my friends and family.

Once I was performing the finger guillotine trick on my great-grandmother (who was in her nineties) and I carelessly didn't set the trick guillotine right. I slammed my hand down on her finger, expecting it to produce the illusion that the blade had magically passed through her finger, but it didn't, and it gave her a gash on the top of her finger. I felt terrible, and from then on I was much more careful to make sure I was setting up the tricks properly.

I would entertain friends and family alike, putting on a show for anyone who would watch.

Those were good days, and I was getting everything I could out of my childhood. One of the things I am most grateful for in those days was how my mother took care of us. My father wasn't terribly involved in our lives but my mom made sure we always had fun outings with the family (at least us kids and her. My dad rarely, if ever, took part). My father mostly yelled at us for various reasons. I recently found a letter I wrote to my dad when I was nine, and it said I was asleep but if he wanted to yell at me for any reason I would be in my room and he could wake me up. My memories of him are of him either sleeping or screaming at us.

My best memories of those days are when we would be allowed to sleep in on school days. There was nothing better than waking up for school to darkness and looking out the window to find out it had snowed, then gathering around in the dull yellow light of the kitchen to listen to the radio to find out if our school was on the list of those closing for a snow day. After the inevitable announcement it was a hot bowl of oatmeal (I still love a hot bowl of oatmeal on snow days), then fourteen layers of clothing, a bread bag over our shoes to keep out the wetness (we were from Texas, we didn't have those rubber shoes that go on the outside of shoes like the northerners do), and out into the snow to play until we couldn't feel our hands and feet.

But those aren't the days I was referring to a minute ago. I was talking about special days that my mother had decided we would have. She would turn off our alarms and when we woke up it would be light outside, meaning something was definitely different. It was a school day, so why did we get to sleep so long? My mom would tell us it was a special day and then she would take all of us kids on an outing somewhere— the Mrs. Baird's Bread factory tour (I can still smell the fresh bread baking), the zoo, a picnic. It didn't matter the occasion, those were the greatest days of my childhood.

I have no idea what motivated my mother to do this, but I can tell you something—if you have the ability to do something like this for your child once or twice a year I cannot recommend more heartily that you do it. There was something about knowing we should have been at school, that we were breaking the rules even though we had our mom's permission, which made it all the more sweet.

The next day she would give us permission slips and we went on with the school year as though nothing had ever happened, but the memories of those wonderful feelings, sights, and smells stayed with us forever. I spent years and years at school and could only tell you a few stories of any of it, but I remember every one of those outings as though they happened yesterday. I think those precious moments will last a lifetime, and I know Debi and Jep feel the same way about those days as I do. Thanks, Mom, for doing that. I only hope this story will inspire others to give their children the same wonderful memories.

I was always small for my age, at least until I got into college, and had to deal with bullies trying to push me around and chase me home after school. I was terrified of them, but I had a plan on how to deal with them.

I had seen the advertisements in my comic books about the skinny guy getting sand kicked in his face, and I had filled out the form. Again, I dreamed of how it would be after I got the magical course in the mail, how I would suddenly be huge and muscular and be able to set those bullies straight. I filled out the order form and wrote in the comment section, 'I'm so weak I couldn't beat up a kitten.' My mother didn't mail it. She kept it for me to see after I grew up. I'll always be grateful for that.

When the Mr. Universe package never showed up, I decided to take up karate. I would learn to defend myself and walk around with the confidence that came with knowing I could defend myself should the need arise. Unfortunately I have never been a patient person and my karate lessons were not giving me the ability to frighten away my tormentors fast enough, so I decided on a new tactic—special effects.

I snapped a two-by-four plank in half and asked my brother to hold it like it was still in one piece. One of the bullies who chased me lived on our street and I waited for him to walk by, and as he did I screamed an ear-bleeding 'Hyyyyeeeahhh!' and hit the board, while Jep masterfully pulled the two pieces apart as though I had broken the plank with my hand.

I don't remember if this little display had any effect on my tormentors since, like all memories, the rest of that story has faded from my consciousness, but I remember quite clearly my effort in trying to scare the bullies by pretending to break a board in half.

The insult I heard most often later came after anyone found out I was a ventriloquist. They would say, 'Which one's the dummy?', after which they would break into howls of laughter as though they had come up with the funniest line ever. This was something I endured almost daily.

I was also the kind of kid who got bored easily and every time we had school pictures taken, I would make a face on one of the shots. Even though the photographers always took more than a dozen shots they always seemed to use that one shot where I had made a face.

In fifth grade I was in the front/center of the group photo and during one of the shots I contorted my face into a frown. As usual the photographer used that one as our class photo. I came in from recess one day and some girls came running up to me and were hitting me and shouting, 'You ruined our class picture! How could you?' I was confused because I had forgotten about pulling the face, but when I got to my desk I saw my enormous frown staring out from the photo.

I was around nine when things started to change with my father. Some of us have parents who descend into darkness and madness, and I guess it is similar in most cases, but when it happens to you the changes happen so subtly and slowly that it is hard to determine when they actually occurred.

Some of these memories are difficult to write about and to even recall, but since they are extremely relevant to who I have become I am going to share them with you.

When I first started doing magic my father seemed amused and enjoyed the tricks, but the better I got at them the less interested he became; in fact, he began to be agitated by them.

He was the one who had introduced me to magic in the first place, but now he became more and more uninterested in my abilities. He would scream at me that I wasn't good enough at a trick, then when I worked hard to get better at it he would lose interest altogether. I became more and more confused by what he wanted or expected from me.

Did he, in fact want me to practice more, or did he want me to give it up? I wanted so desperately to have him tell me I had gotten really good at magic, so I doubled my efforts to be better. I practiced every waking moment, flashing cards here and there, producing coins from thin air and making them vanish just as easily. I could fan entire decks of cards with each hand, then shuffle and cut each one single-handedly.

I was almost ten when he came home and announced that I had become obsessed with being a magician and would no longer be allowed to do it. He then took all of my magic props away and threw them in the trash. End of story. I was devastated to say the least. I had spent so much time getting good at performing magic and now it was all gone.

It was difficult to understand why he did this, but when I was older he confided to me that he had always wanted to be a performer, but had never had the courage to pursue the dream. I am convinced to this day that jealousy was his main motivation. I think that he couldn't bear the thought that his nine-year-old son was better at something than he was, so he put an end to it.

It is inconceivable to me how any parent could be so jealous of their children to actually sabotage them so they wouldn't out-succeed them. I have no children myself, possibly because of the way my father treated us children since we were very young, constantly reminding us of what a burden we had been and how much better his life would have been if we had never come along. We were nothing but trouble and it would have been better if we had never been born, according to him. I have been able to deal with a lot of the emotional scars my father inflicted upon me, but I have never had even the slightest desire to have children. However, I do get a lot of satisfaction knowing how much children enjoy my work and that is definitely a blessing in my life.

In spite of the fact that I have no children I truly cannot comprehend actually wanting my children (if I had any) to fail. I know that this is exactly what my father wanted. The idea that any of his children would succeed beyond what he had accomplished (which wasn't and isn't much since he is not motivated and has never even tried to do anything with his life) was totally unacceptable and he would see to it that we would fail. He began a long and dark descent into insanity, jealousy, and bitterness, which has led to a permanent separation from all of his children and family.

My dad began to force us kids to do things that he was interested in. He started running; therefore we kids had to join in. In spite of the fact that I was about a third his size he demanded that I keep up pace with him and would run us several miles until we couldn't breathe. Once after a run I collapsed on the grass gasping for air and he punished me by forcing me to run another few miles.

This went on for months until he lost interest in running, then we all got to quit. To this day I cannot exercise because of those horrific torturous memories of being pushed mercilessly beyond my limits and getting no sympathy from my father. He also got on a kick of eating large spoonfuls of bran and would force us kids to eat a spoonful as well; if we gagged we got spanked.

It was a slow progression, but things got worse and worse as we got older.

As is true in many stories of very talented individuals, an enormous amount of my motivation lay in the idea that I would make my father proud. Like Alice in Wonderland I endlessly pursued the elusive white rabbit. My father's praise and admiration lay just around the next corner; I was forever hoping that if I just got a little bit better he would finally admit that he was proud of me.

But I never caught the rabbit. It was only after I gave up the chase that I was able to find true freedom and a sense of pride in my accomplishments, but once again, I am getting ahead of my story.

So here I was, a nine-year-old who had his dream destroyed suddenly, and had no idea what to do with his free time.

At that stage in my life my dad suddenly became very religious and decided to throw away everything in the house that did not revolve around religion. All books, records, paintings, anything that was not a part of his new religious philosophy had to go, so we purged the house.

I decided that the way to my father's heart must surely be through religion, so I dived in head-first (as I always tend to do) and became a child preacher. I would set my alarm clock for 5am and get up and walk to our church in the darkness (about two miles) to pray. Sometimes my dad would accompany me, sometimes not.

I would take my dad's huge Zondervan Bible and ride the bus to downtown Dallas to preach on the street corner.

For a little while it did feel like my father was proud, but it was short-lived. What my dad didn't know was that Jefferies Magicland was downtown, and when I took my breaks from preaching to passers-by, I would head over to the shop to dream of performing illusions once again. I'd buy small tricks and keep them hidden from my dad so he wouldn't take them away again, then I would go back out on the streets to preach some more.

I never felt the call of God to preach; I just wanted my dad to be proud of me, but once again the rabbit got away and disappeared down the hole, uncaught, taunting me with his elusiveness.

When I was ten, I was given an assignment at school (Northlake Elementary School in Richardson, Texas) to write a report on Valentine's Day. Thank goodness for the Dewey Decimal System, since without it I may never have found my true calling. If we had had the computer systems of today's libraries, I don't think it would have happened.

You see, while flipping through the card catalogues I overshot the VAs (for Valentine's Day) and landed on the VEs, specifically on Ventriloquism. There it was, staring at me, the name of a book: *Ventriloquism for Fun & Profit* by Paul Winchell. The idea of doing ventriloquism intrigued me. I had several years earlier, ordered the mouth prop advertised in comic books that would allow me to 'Fool Your Friends!' and showed a picture of a guy standing next to a closet with a voice saying 'Let me out!' coming from it. A girl was standing next to him with an astonished look on her face.

Once again, as I had many times before, I imagined all of the scenarios I would be in as I placed the magical item in my mouth and could suddenly make voices come from all over the place. It turned out to be a little thing you put in your mouth that helped you do bird-calls, plus a crappy book on how to do ventriloquism. And, as before, I was disappointed, but merrily moved onto my next project.

But this was different. It was an actual manual on how to do ventriloquism. It showed the detailed technique of how to throw your voice, and even how to build your own puppet.

I eagerly checked the book out, completely forgetting about my assignment on Valentine's Day and raced home after school, excited to learn my new art form.

I had no idea how that day was to change my life.

Chapter 3

A Boy and His Doll

I was a little wary about starting a whole new project, since I knew that I may spend several years developing it and my father might just yank it away from me, as he had my magic act. But I had a plan.

I was going for a 'two-fer', a phrase we have in Texas that means you kill two birds with one stone.

I would tell my dad that I wanted to be a ventriloquist as a part of my ministry, therefore there was no way he could possibly object to my doing it.

Just as I suspected, he thought it was a great idea, and I began to save my money to buy my own vent puppet. My plan was that I would only rehearse when he wasn't around, so he would never think I was obsessed with it.

Every chance I had I'd practice saying my alphabet without moving my lips. I found that I had a natural knack for doing it and would try my hardest to make my ventriloquial voice as clear as I could.

After a couple of weeks I finally had enough money to buy my first puppet, since my mom had told me she would pay for half of the $20 I needed, and I bought a little vent doll from Sears called 'Willie Talk'. It was a vent figure (as we in the vent world call our hard traditional ventriloquist puppets), that only had a string coming out of the back of his neck that opened his mouth. I was unable to move his head or any other part of his face, but it was enough.

I started to do little shows for the family and especially my mom, who was the exact opposite of my dad in that she was a veritable fountain of encouragement. She decided to help me out and work on 'Josh' to make him a little more professional. (I had named my first character Josh because I thought it was a clever play on words, Josh being short for Joshua and also another name for a joke. Not bad for a ten-year-old, huh?) My mom took him apart and, using bits from my sister Debi's dolls, fixed his eyes so I could close them, put a wig on him and built him an entirely new body out of a milk jug, and glued a stick to his head so I could turn it. So now I had a semi-professional vent figure (at least it seemed that way to me) and no material.

I started to write routines for Terry & Josh, the name I gave my act. I wrote several skits with me and Josh, and put on a performance for my family about a month after I had started doing ventriloquism. I had sprinkled Bible stories among the jokes I wrote so my father would approve.

My mother went on and on about how good I was and how amazing my abilities were, and when I asked my dad what he thought he said, 'You're a terrible writer. You can't write—so don't even try. I think from now on you should buy your material and not worry about writing again.'

It's amazing how one little statement can cause years of grief and trouble. My subconscious mind latched onto this with a vengeance and for many years I simply could not write. It was only after I did a very intensive self-hypnosis therapy session that I was able to break the spell my father put on me that day.

In spite of the fact that my dad didn't think I could write, he couldn't deny the talent I had. I was able to talk without moving my lips within just a few days of reading the book, but since my dad hated my writing, he ordered some dialogue books from Maher Ventriloquist Studios.

It absolutely boggles my mind that anyone could think a ten-year-old should be a professional writer, but I began to understand his logic later on when he told me that he believed that natural talent meant a person could do something without practice. He actually thinks that if someone can't pick up a guitar for the first time and instantly play like Eddie Van Halen, it means they don't have talent. He has said this very thing to me as an adult, so I know he believes it.

He felt the same thing about my brother after he started to play guitar. He constantly told my brother he had no talent for the guitar even though Jep Jr worked diligently at it and became quite good, good enough in fact to play in my band several years later, but since he actually had to practice, my father felt that he had no talent.

To this day my brother thinks he's not a good guitar player, but he is really very talented and if you ever hear him play you'll agree, but alas, the psychological poison fed to children all too often saturates our psyche and destroys our self-confidence permanently. I hope one day Jep accepts the facts, and lets his true talent blossom

Even though my dad's stupidity was the reason I had them, the dialogue books were a true godsend. I was able to comb them and pick out my favorite jokes and cull together a thirty-minute routine. I did it for my family and they loved it. I was ready to start my new career.

As I was putting together my first routines I found out about a puppeteering convention that was to be held in the Dallas area. My mom told me she would take me to it.

I was so excited and I wandered around all day, checking out the puppets and dialogue books for sale. I even bought a bag of balloons to make animal balloons with and a book teaching me how to do it. I used those for years (until I ran out of them), doing shows for birthday parties and other events, finishing the show with balloon animals. Hey, an entertainer always looks for ways to entertain!

The highlight of the convention was a performance by an up-and-coming teenage ventriloquist named Jeff Dunham. I watched eagerly as he did his act, which included a 'nose blowing' routine (where the dummy would need his nose blown and the ventriloquist would oblige, then the dummy would end up blowing his nose along the entire arm of the ventriloquist), which I promptly decided to 'borrow', and then the finale: he closed the suitcase on his dummy Monty's leg and made him scream from within the case. It was amazing! I also 'borrowed' the closing-case-on-the-leg routine (hey, give me a break, I was ten. I didn't even know what plagiarism was back then). So now I had a couple of really good routines (albeit written by Jeff Dunham) to include in my act. I even had a closer!

After the show I went up and met Jeff. I told him I was just starting to do ventriloquism and he invited me to come over and see his workshop. I was so excited I could hardly stand it. My mom took me over to his house and he showed me where he built his dummies, and then showed me how to drink a glass of water while making the dummy talk.

It was one of the most gracious things anyone has ever done in my life, and I have repaid the favor by showing the same hospitality to any new vents out there I have met throughout my career.

He has since gone on to become one of the most popular ventriloquists around and I am always so happy to hear about his success. Thanks, Jeff, for being such a great guy! You have no idea how much you inspired me.

I joined the North American Association of Ventriloquists (yes, an organization like that once existed!) and started to receive their newsletter, cleverly titled *Newsy Vents*. The first issue I received had a picture on the cover of another ventriloquist on it that I would come to idolize throughout my career, Ronn Lucas. I eagerly read the article about Ronn, about how he played at mall openings, (I fantasized about performing in front of a couple of dozen people in the middle of a mall), cruise ships, and other such venues.

That was it. The dream of becoming a professional ventriloquist had just been born in me like a bug, wriggling inside me with its insatiable appetite, forever longing for more and more attention. I craved to do what Jeff Dunham and Ronn Lucas did. I was determined that one day I would do it.

I had read about a ventriloquist convention in Fort Mitchell, KY in my *Newsy Vents* newsletter and began to dream of someday going there, but year after year I had to miss it. First I was too young, and then when I got old enough I was never able to take time off work to go. I decided in my late thirties that I would just wait until I was well-known enough to be asked to come. It seemed like that day would never come so I just put it out of my head and continued to work. After *America's Got Talent* I received an invitation from the head of the convention, so it was just one more lifelong dream that had come true thanks to the show.

Oops, I have jumped ahead to my late thirties, but I guess now I need to get back to my ten-year-old self.

In the time it took me to get the books and learn the new routine, memorize it and get comfortable enough to perform it, I had turned eleven, but I felt I was ready to take my new act to the public.

My mom arranged for me to be the sole entertainment for the July 4, 1976 Bicentennial celebration picnic at Forest Meadow Baptist Church in Richardson, Texas. This was it! My first real-paying show. I was to be paid $25 for entertaining.

I was a hit! Everyone raved about how talented I was and how they couldn't believe that I could do that at only eleven years old. I was ecstatic! I made the decision that I wanted to do this as a career, and the dream of being a professional ventriloquist was born. I began to dream of the day I would set the world on fire and become the next Edgar Bergen.

What? You've never heard of Edgar Bergen? Why, he's only the most famous ventriloquist of all time! He was a huge hit in the days of Vaudeville and had his own radio show (*The Charlie McCarthy Show*) for almost twenty years! Charlie McCarthy was his most popular character, but Mortimer Snerd was a close second. Many folks thought it was amazing that a ventriloquist became so popular on the radio but it was because Edgar created great characters, something I have always tried to emulate. On a side note, Candice Bergen is his daughter and she found her own fame as a movie actor, and with the television show *Murphy Brown* and more recently on *Boston Legal*.

I say that everyone raved about my first show. That is an exaggeration. One person didn't like it very much. Any guess who? My father berated me for every mistake, telling me that I didn't really have any talent at it, but that I could pass as a ventriloquist if I would take his suggestions, which I eagerly did. Once again that pesky white rabbit was within arm's reach, and all I had to do was follow my dad's every suggestion and he would be mine!

I faithfully made notes and changed every part of my act to my father's whims, but alas, he never praised my efforts. I was only met, show after show, with a whole new list of suggestions and demands. I faithfully obliged each demand and honed my craft ever onward, getting better and better, but feeling that I was making no progress because the one person I longed to impress, never was.

I made two appearances on a local Dallas area television show called *Peppermint Place* over the span of that year, but nothing I did ever brought praise from my dad. He berated me for my lack of ad lib abilities. I sometimes didn't have a clever enough comeback when asked something and he would go on and on to me about how I couldn't ad lib so I should always just stick to the script. As a result, instead of working on my ad libs I cowered away from them, terrified anytime something unexpected happened in the show or someone asked me a question during an interview.

Again, my father had planted seeds of doubt in my mind that took decades to weed out of my psyche. It was only after years of learning to relax and let the humor of the situation come to me that I mastered the ability to not get flustered in unexpected situations.

But as a kid I never felt I was making any progress as an entertainer even though I spent every waking available moment practicing.

Recently I did a show in Corsicana, Texas, a city where I spent several years as a youth, and before I went on, the organizers surprised me with a video of me at fourteen years old performing in a local revue. I was truly stunned at how good I was at that age. I honestly believed that I didn't become really good at ventriloquism until I was in my thirties because that was when my father finally cut off from me and I didn't have to deal with his criticism.

I had no idea that at fourteen I was already one of the best ventriloquists around; I thought I was a no-talent hack who was simply struggling to be as good as I could. Isn't it funny how we see ourselves through the eyes of those who criticized us when we were young?

I remember seeing a photocopy of a contract in one of the ventriloquism books I had collected that listed $500 as the price the ventriloquist was receiving for his show at a club. I would stare at that contract for hours and dream of the day I might actually be able to make that much for my craft, all the while rehearsing and practicing in secret, terrified that my father would decide I was obsessed with ventriloquism and take it away from me as he had my magic act.

I was using my ventriloquism now in every aspect of my life. I would perform at church for the other children and then I would do my act for the talent show at school. My mom also took out a little ad for me in a small community newspaper to do birthday party entertainment.

I was in the sixth grade and I decided to run for president of the school board. I have no idea why because I have never since been interested in becoming a politician, but there I was, developing a campaign that featured me running for school board president. We utilized my being a ventriloquist as best we could. We put out a poster with a picture of me and Josh that said, 'Don't be a dummy. Vote for Terry Fator!' Luckily a kid who looked like he would one day run for the Senate actually won the election and I to this day believed the best man won, but it shows how I was using my ventriloquism all the time.

Of course, I also used it in other ways. For example, I could talk to my friends during class without moving my lips, making it very difficult for the teachers to tell who was doing the talking. They eventually figured it out, and soon I was getting blamed pretty much any time anyone talked out of turn.

I would also go to the local department store and hang out in the luggage section, trying to fool everyone into believing that there were people trapped in the suitcases. I can't remember if anyone actually fell for it, but a friend of mine did when we were going door-to-door selling candy for school.

We had arrived at a house that looked empty. My friend knocked at the door and I used ventriloquism to say, 'I'll be right there!'

We waited patiently until he knocked again. 'Just a second!' the voice inside yelled.

We continued to wait for about ten more minutes before my friend finally realized that it had been me all along, and we laughed hard at the joke. I loved it when we got back to school and he told the story to all our friends, and once again I was where I belonged, the center of attention, with everyone asking me to make voices come out of every closet in the school.

Recently my wife and I were at Chicago's Shedd Aquarium and there was a bunch of kids crowded around a display containing a large sea turtle, which was scratching against the glass right in front of the children. I was standing there and suddenly I made a voice come from inside the glass saying, 'Help! Let me out of here!' The kids were so excited to hear a turtle talking. I never told them it was me. I know that for years they are going to insist they heard a turtle talk. (Winston the Impersonating Turtle loves that story!)

I spent a lot of time playing jokes on folks, a couple of times proudly restraining myself at funerals of relatives. The temptation was just about unbearable to have a voice come out of the casket, but I never succumbed to the temptation to do that.

Even though I loved to play good-natured jokes on people using my ventriloquism, I had a very large heart even as a young boy. My sister Debi and I would frequently knock on the doors of any new neighbors that had moved near us and welcome them to our neighborhood. If they had children we would befriend them so they would immediately have friends in their new environment. I also made sure to seek out any children at school who seemed lonely and would make sure to spend time with them so they didn't have to be by themselves. I was constantly trying to befriend the friendless, and it kept me very busy.

In spite of all this, I never stopped working on my act. I would read every dialogue book I had, trying to find any joke that might be funny and would work for me. It was during this time that I began to develop my direction as a comedian.

I started to realize that I didn't enjoy just randomly telling joke after joke, like a typical ventriloquist. I had a lot more fun placing each joke so that it fitted into a certain category. For example, I would mention to Josh that I noticed he had a dog. I would then structure the next few jokes to be about his dog and dog ownership.

I would block all the jokes together to be about subjects that might come up in actual conversation, and eventually I eliminated all the silly jokes altogether, in lieu of comic situations based on Josh's character. This was very difficult to do, but I liked it better. I had begun to analyze my favorite TV sitcoms and jokes, trying to understand why I thought them funny. I liked situational humor much more. I loved *The Munsters*, not because of any jokes they might tell, but because Fred Gwynne's Herman Munster was funny in and of itself.

I wouldn't just watch the shows for entertainment, although I did enjoy them; I would pick apart every sitcom and analyze why I thought a particular line or bit was funny to me. I would then try to adapt that type of humor to my act.

During this time my father had taken an interest in my abilities as a ventriloquist and was giving me advice, albeit terrible advice, on my performances. I had taken my favorite jokes from all of the dialogue books I had, and put a show together that incorporated Bible stories and jokes to make quite an entertaining little routine, but it was never good enough for my dad. Either it was too funny and not religious enough or it was too religious and not funny enough. I struggled to find exactly what it was he wanted from me, but again, I was never able to determine it because all of my hard work only served to produce another long laundry list of things I needed to improve.

Apart from my father's constant criticism I was analyzing my act through my own eyes as well. I noticed that Josh didn't look real enough when he talked. I would stare at myself in the mirror and watch how when I turned my head I would move my eyes right and left as well. I determined that when I had a figure that moved its eyes right and left I would make sure they did it like a real human does. I wanted people to get lost in the illusion that Josh was a real character and not a dummy. I was determined to make sure he was as real as possible.

The one thing I could count on was that any expression of religion would bring praise and admiration from my dad, so I spent a lot of time trying to make sure my dad knew that I wanted to use my talents to preach to others.

I don't want to give the impression that I had no heart for using my gifts to tell Bible stories; I am just now admitting even to myself that it never was a calling. Some feel compelled to go into the ministry and consider it a call from God, and perhaps it is. I never felt that call; I did it purely because I knew it was the only way to be sure my father never took ventriloquism away from me.

To my father, being a minister was the highest calling on earth, just so long as that minister believed everything *he* believed. The second any minister said anything even remotely contrary to something my dad believed, we packed up and moved churches. The pressure to live up to my father's expectations was enormous, and independent thought was not tolerated in any way, shape or form.

The confusion of having to not only move from school to school but also from church to church can take a heavy emotional toll on a child. Every friend I had made was forever gone and I had to start over from scratch every few months. I don't know if my father will ever understand what he actually did to us children through his behavior in not simply accepting that people have differing opinions and that everyone's opinions are as valid as his. I cannot fathom how all three of my father's children ended up tolerant, decent, loving people, but somehow we were able to overcome our dad's extreme narcissism and care about those around us.

I have a very difficult time making new friends to this day, but once I make a friend it is for life. It was a regular practice of my parents to cut friends out of their lives when they did or said anything my parents disagreed with, and I am thankful that I don't have that trait. Maybe it's because so many of my friends were taken from me without my consent that I am reluctant to make new ones, but I hold on to friends for dear life once they have gotten into my heart.

I really did (and still do) love God but I truly felt that He had called me to make people laugh, and still believe that to this very day. The very idea that God could ever call anyone to a task other than trying to promote my father's religious views was utterly ridiculous to him. Everything my dad believed was right and true—and anyone who felt differently was just deluded, and needed to be set straight, and I was to be the vessel God would use to teach everyone the right way to believe.

It's difficult to admit to myself that I used religion for selfish purposes, but my consolation is the fact that it was the only choice I had if I wanted to pursue my dream—so I embraced it enthusiastically. I even went so far as to write sermons and preach at whatever church we happened to be attending then, and it was just about the only time I ever received praise from my father. My heart wasn't in it for the glory of God, I only hoped that the elusive white rabbit (my father's approval) could finally be mine. But the whole point of the white rabbit is that he is never caught. How can a young mind comprehend that? So much of our youth can be wasted in the pursuit of something that is unattainable, but I had many years to go before I would learn that valuable lesson.

I was getting better and better as a ventriloquist, even though it didn't feel like I was making any progress. Unlike my father, my mum was always full of praise so I continued to work as hard as I could, hoping that one day Dad would be proud.

You may notice that there aren't many other people mentioned in this story so far. As I sat and reflected on my youth I was amazed at how little I remembered any close friends—and I was shocked to realize why. My family was constantly moving. We never stayed at any one location for more than a few months. A lot of military children experience this type of life, but we were not military; we just moved all the time.

It's strange to me to hear stories from my wife about her school years because she grew up in the same area and went to the same schools her friends went to year after year. I think my parents burned a lot of bridges because we always left an area and never again had anything to do with the people we left behind, but this is just conjecture since I really have no idea about the reason.

We adapt so quickly when we are children, so all of my best friends were quickly forgotten in lieu of the new ones we were forced to make as we started a whole new life at whatever school we were attending at the time. I'm sure Debi and Jep had the same trouble. We compensated for the lack of any lasting friendships by turning to each other, the only constant in our young lives, and to this day we remain much closer than most siblings.

As I stated before, I still have trouble developing lasting relationships, and I think it's because I had no practice at it growing up.

Anyway, back to the story of my life. I continued to work as much as I could as a ventriloquist, and when I was eleven I got a booking at a VFW event (VFW standing for Veterans of Foreign Wars). I got up to entertain and did my show. The audience loved it! They were cheering and hollering for more, so the emcee got up and took the microphone from me. 'Did y'all enjoy that?' he screamed. The audience went wild.

As an eleven-year-old who was raised in a Christian home, I don't think I had ever encountered an intoxicated adult before, and this one was a doozy! The emcee was smashed, so he got up and proceeded to barrage me with questions.

This would have been fine, but he would also ask questions of Josh, my dummy, and when he did he would put the mike in front of Josh so the audience couldn't hear anything he said. Of course, this could have just been a testament of how good *I* was, since Jerry Springer on *America's Got Talent* would do the same thing. In fact, after the first episode the producers would always mike me with a lavalier so the audience could hear the puppets. Jerry never figured it out and I know for a fact that he wasn't drunk, but I know that the emcee of my first VFW show was quite inebriated.

We all had a good laugh about it on the way home, and I continued to try to improve as much as I could so my dad would praise me.

I hired an agent out of the Dallas, Texas, area and she would send me to various auditions, once at a bar having its own 'Gong Show' and I came in second place, losing to a belly dancer. I was a clueless little kid but I was smart enough even then to know why I lost that one.

I continued to do many auditions for commercials and other things, once auditioning to be in *The Bad News Bears Go to Japan*. I had not seen any of the movies but was aware that the kids in the movies swore a lot, so I walked up to do the audition and announced that I wanted the part, but under no circumstances would I ever say a curse word. I didn't get the part.

No matter how much I auditioned I never got much work, but I was still busy doing birthday parties and, of course, school work and other kid stuff.

I longed to be famous because I knew that then my father would have to admit I was talented. I kept trying and dreaming, working as often as I could when I was alone, so as not to arouse any suspicion from my dad that I was obsessing over my new career.

Eventually he began to complain that I wasn't practicing enough. 'I never see you rehearse. You need to get on the ball if you ever want to be great at ventriloquism,' he would shout.

I wasn't fooled, though. My father would change his mind so quickly and violently that I knew not to trust him in this. He had done the exact same thing about my magic. He griped that I wasn't working hard enough on it, and once I finally started to, he yanked it out of my life. There was no way I was going to let him do it again.

To this day I don't like anyone around when I rehearse. My wife has told people for several years that I don't practice, but she only thinks that because she has never seen me do it. Any time I'm alone I still do scales and practice my distant voice (the voice I use when I 'throw' my voice). I have always loved to rehearse; I just do it alone.

I was diligently working on my act and on my skills, and I was getting more and more church shows.

Things really changed in our lives when I was twelve. My parents had decided that they were tired of working for others so they started a janitorial business, with the three of us kids as the only employees. I hated it, but I also credit it with my ability to work hard and take real pride in doing a good job, no matter what it is I am doing.

But it also meant effectively an end to my childhood. From the moment my parents decided to have a family business we kids went to work full-time, and except for a few occasions over the next few years, we were full-time workers.

From then on during school months we would attend school, and then go to a building to clean it, then on home to do our homework, and off to bed, repeating this routine day after tedious day

The summer months were far worse. My dad would drop us off with two thousand flyers and we would spend every day walking miles and miles of neighborhoods all over the Dallas area trying to drum up business. We would offer carpet cleaning and painting, anything anyone needed us to do. And when the flyers worked and we got hired we would have to go to the houses and provide whatever services we had been hired for.

Eventually my folks got a contract with a couple of apartment buildings and we would work sometimes up to sixty hours straight with no sleep because we had thirty or forty apartments that needed to be finished by the end of a weekend.

It was during these times that I discovered another true joy—old-time radio programs. During those long thirty-plus hour marathon work weekends, our local radio station would play radio shows in the late night hours, everything from *Lum and Abner* to *The Charlie McCarthy Show*. Hour after tedious hour would fly by as we devoured episodes of *The Shadow* and *The Lone Ranger*. Fibber McGee and Molly were our constant companions as we toiled, and they were welcome visitors.

Jep, Debi and I would listen to them together as we cleaned apartment after apartment, the paint-covered radio blasting out at all hours of the night, and we still remember some of our favorite shows to this very day.

There was an episode of some suspense show about a baby that ate and ate and grew to be the size of a large adult in a couple of days that we will never forget. The sound of the baby scarfing down its food was hilarious, and we laughed long into the night at it. Even though it was difficult, we always had each other's company and that was a blessing. Always the comedian, I would have my brother and sister in stitches, using whatever I could to get a laugh, and the laughter made the days bearable.

I also began to use the endless hours of cleaning buildings and apartments to practice my ventriloquism. When I was alone (as we were for hours at a time) cleaning an entire floor of a building by myself, while Jep and Debi and my mom would be cleaning their own floors, I would practice saying the alphabet without moving my lips. Then I discovered that I could entertain myself and practice my ventriloquism at the same time by singing along with music that was playing without moving my lips. I would sing for hours, all the while keeping my lips as still as I could so I could practice my diction, the hard letters (P, B, and M), and have fun all at once. I could never have dreamed that I was training for something that would one day capture the hearts of the entire country.

I had read in an article of *Newsy Vents* that practice was the key to becoming great at ventriloquism. The writer of the article recounted how he had once met a great ventriloquist (I can't remember who) and he had asked him the secret to his success. The pro vent said 'practice'.

'I knew you'd say that,' the writer said. He was impressed that the ventriloquist had said the word 'practice' perfectly without moving his lips.

I never forgot that article and I always wanted to be able to do the same so I started to say the word 'practice' without moving my lips, no small feat. If you think it's easy, try it right now. See what I mean? It's very difficult to do, but I used those endless hours of cleaning and emptying trash and scrubbing floors to rehearse it until I could say it perfectly just like the ventriloquist in the story.

I was twelve and going into the seventh grade when my parents decided that the public school system was a bad idea and that we could not be raised in such a bastion of evil. They decided to put us in a Christian school.

My first experience with this new schooling was Garland Christian Academy in Garland, Texas. We couldn't afford the tuition so my parents made a deal with the school that we kids would clean it at the end of every school day in lieu of money, and they accepted the deal.

Can you imagine what it was like to be the janitor for the school you go to? As difficult as it is to feel accepted by your peers as a regular kid, it is far worse when you have to clean the school. Not only did we have to endure the jokes and belittling, but we never were able to feel like we fitted in. Kids can be cruel anyway, but when you give them so much ammunition it can feel unbearable at times. I learned during those years to become isolated emotionally and develop a tough heart that didn't care if I was liked or not. At least I thought I had done that. The truth is that I desperately wanted to be popular, but it wasn't to be. Maybe that's why I craved fame for so many years. Maybe I was longing for the acceptance of my peers for so long that I hoped one day I would get it from strangers.

It wasn't the worst experience, but I never felt like a part of the school. It was comprised of mostly students that had gone to Lavon Drive Baptist Church together since they were babies, and the sense of isolation for us was really strong. I was also starting puberty and was noticing girls in a way I never had before, but I was ignored completely by them all. I was especially in love with Becky, the pastor's daughter and a cheerleader, and who was far and away the most beautiful girl I had ever seen. I longed for her to notice me, but to no avail. I must not have made any impression at all because several years later I saw her at college and she didn't even remember me.

Between going to school, cleaning the school, then being picked up by our parents and having to go out and clean a building or two before going home and doing my homework, I had no time to work on my ventriloquism. I would try to go over new routines and practice my alphabet ventriloquially while at work cleaning. It was during these long hard years that I determined that I didn't want anything to do with manual labour when I grew up. I began to dream ever more fervently of the day I could become a professional ventriloquist, always visualising that contract for $500 I had seen in the book. That was more than we got paid to clean a whole apartment building, and that was just for forty-five minutes worth of entertaining in a club. I was determined to get out of this life of constant working.

In spite of how difficult these days were, I have very fond memories of them. I absolutely loved the radio shows in the middle of the night, and my mom made sure to always try to make things fun for us. My father rarely worked, preferring to go home and rest while we did the jobs he had been hired to do, always taking the time to scream at us for not doing the job as well as he would have if he had done it himself.

On the harder days we would go to a steak house for lunch and get these huge chicken fried steaks the size of large plates and would eat until we were bursting. Those were good times, and they tend to stand out in my memory far stronger that the difficulties we faced.

But just around the corner were some of the most challenging years of my life. I would become a teenager, and while I found some new experiences that gave my life meaning, I also went through the emotional angst most of us feel during those years.

Chapter 4
I was a Teenage Ventriloquist

I had entered a new age. Pimples and pain were to be the order of the next decade.

I discovered an intense loneliness as I became interested in girls. At first it was because they did not reciprocate at all, but as I got older and a girl here or there would show some interest, my parents began to put the clamps down on my love life and would refuse to allow me to have anything to do with them.

The idea of having a girlfriend was utterly ridiculous in the Fator household. Teenagers simply did not date, and that was that.

My father had a very short temper and had emotionally abused us since we were very young. Screaming and belittling was the order of the household and as much as we hated it, it was our life, and there was not much option but to accept it.

Some listen to what is being told to them as children by abusive fathers and some rebel. I was the latter and refused to accept the things he said about me. Even though I felt lazy since I heard it from him on a daily basis, I didn't want to be lazy so I worked hard to not be. It was the same about being stupid. Being told you are stupid year after year can make you feel that's what you are, but since I didn't want to be stupid, I worked hard to be smart.

When my father told me something couldn't be done I would set out to prove him wrong. He told me that I could never be a puppeteer as good as The Muppets, so I worked as hard as I could to show him he was wrong.

I simply refused to lay back and give in to what my father told me I was. Being hard-headed I wouldn't accept that I couldn't do something simply because he said so.

He told me many times as I grew up that he would break my spirit like a strong-willed horse, and even though I would outwardly go along with what he wanted, inside I would determine to do things my own way, and usually it turned out better for me. I was improving as a ventriloquist exponentially because I decided that I wanted to be the best in the world. My father continued to tell me I was no good, but passable. I accepted his conclusion, and it made me work that much harder.

I think a lot of the time people don't understand that they have been physically abused until they become adults, simply because for them the abuse was a normal part of life and we assume that everyone else has had the same type of life as ours.

My sister and I were talking a few years back and had the realization that we had been physically abused as far back as we remembered, but had not realized it because my dad only spanked us on our butts.

Only once did he hit me across the face; I was eight, and he hit me so hard I flew across the room. I was standing on the bed eating crackers at the time and Debi, who watched the whole thing, tells me that it seemed like slow motion as crackers flew out of my mouth and I sailed to the wall and crashed into it.

The other times my father punished us was on our bottoms, but he would spank us so hard and with such force that our butts and thighs would turn every shade of color that is unnatural on a human body and it would literally be a week before we could sit down without pain.

As is always the way in these cases, my father made sure we dressed so the terrible bruises all down the backs of our legs couldn't be seen by anyone else. It wasn't their business, you see. What happened in our house was between us only. I think we assumed the other kids had the same bruises and we never really talked about it to anyone.

I know that my mother suffered to see us being treated this way, but in those days there were no support groups for folks in our situation. We just took it and moved on. My father was a frightening person, especially to a child, but almost as much to a woman who had had her own self-image shredded by her own father.

I am telling you all this to explain why we simply didn't date. We were terrified of my father and his wrath. He could explode at the drop of a hat and take his anger out on any of us, so we were very careful to not disobey him.

I felt so lonely and longed for one of the girls I had a crush on to hold my hand or show me some sort of affection, but fear of my dad kept me from pursuing the feelings in any way.

When I was thirteen, my parents moved us to Lewisville Christian Academy in Lewisville, Texas, and we were introduced to a whole new curriculum, A.C.E. or Accelerated Christian Education. It was based on students working at their own pace and level of intelligence, and it was perfect for me.

I have always been ADD, although we had no term for it when I was young. I found it very difficult to concentrate at the pace of the other students in the class and my mind would wander incessantly. I was a straight B and C student until I got into A.C.E.; school was never much of a problem for me after that. My grades were better and I was much happier, if very lonely.

I guess it's hard for parents to understand what is going on in their kids' lives. I suppose mine were only trying to protect me from making a mistake, but I also think it was the absolute insistence that we were not allowed to make our own mistakes that caused a lot of the emotional trouble I had to deal with in my young life.

One of the ways I was able to keep my sense of self was to find small ways to disobey my father as often as I could, just so I could feel that I had my own identity and wasn't being absorbed into my father's personality like a Borg. (Sorry, my geekiness just reared its head. A Borg is a character from *Star Trek: The Next Generation* that absorbs the uniqueness of individuals and turns them into a hive-mind mentality.)

My dad had decided that watching television was wrong for us kids but OK for himself. We had a television but he had cut the power cord off it and had fixed a cord that would plug into the wall and the cut end as well. He thought he had us, but we went to Radio Shack and bought a power cord, making our own special cord that allowed us to watch television whenever my parents were out of the house, which was pretty much every night.

We would watch all the popular shows of the day like *Happy Days, Laverne and Shirley, Diff'rent Stokes* and *Facts of Life*, allowing us to join in the conversations of our friends at school as they discussed the latest episodes of their favorite shows. Any time we watched television this way, we would take turns at the watch, keeping one eye on the TV and the other on the window to see if the family car had turned into our driveway. Believe me, we had some close calls when the person who was supposed to be watching got too involved in a program and suddenly realized that the car was in the driveway and our parents were on their way in. We never did get caught, though, and it is one of my favorite memories—Jep, Debi and I watching our favorite shows coupled with the thrill of doing something forbidden and not getting caught doing it.

Things began to change when we moved the next year to yet another school, Mesquite Christian Academy in Mesquite, Texas. Luckily it was also an A.C.E. school and I was able to continue to excel in my schooling, at least the part I wanted to excel in. I have never had patience to force myself to do something I don't enjoy, so since I loved English and science I did quite well in those subjects, but I hated math and social studies, so I fell farther and farther behind in those subjects.

But something happened, changing my mind about all that. I found out that the A.C.E. schools had a national competition, and one of the categories was ventriloquism. The only hitch was that I had to be up to date in all of my subjects in order to be eligible. Within a week I was completely caught up. I discovered that with a little motivation I was capable of anything.

I competed in the regionals, which included all of Texas, and I won, which meant I got to go to Chattanooga, Tennessee, to compete in the nationals and represent my whole state. I had the time of my life. It was the first opportunity I'd had to do anything apart from my parents, and it was bliss. I found that I could think outside of the family unit and that I could be clever, too!

I wrote a routine that incorporated the 'distant voice' into my act. It was the first time in the history of the competition anyone had done that. The skit was one where Josh confessed to a number of situations where he had been bad, with comic results of course, and it ended with him receiving a phone call from an angel telling him that God wanted him to repent and start living a better life. The judges raved about the originality of the routine and I won the nationals competition, hands down.

The following year I won regionals again and headed to Rutgers University to compete in the nationals once more.

This year I wrote a routine involving Josh as Daniel, and I used a lion puppet I had as one of the lions from the Bible story of Daniel in the lions' den.

I told the story from both perspectives, having Daniel describe how he would never compromise his convictions, and had the lion tell about how an angel had appeared to him and his friends and told them, although they were very hungry, not to eat Daniel. Of course, they obeyed.

Again the judges raved on and on about the originality of the routine and I won easily, even though about five or six of the other ventriloquists used the 'distant voice' in their routines because it had worked so well for me the year before.

Winning the competition meant a lot to me, but not as much as what happened to me the last night I was in New Jersey.

A lovely young lady I had met the night before and I were talking and I mentioned that I would be fifteen soon and had never kissed a girl. She assured me that she would see to it that I had kissed a girl before my next birthday and proceeded to make sure she kept her promise by taking it upon herself to fulfill it. She pulled me into the bushes and laid one on me. My hormones and emotions exploded! I had never before known the wonder of contact of any kind with the opposite sex, and I liked it. I liked it a lot. After the first kiss ended she said to me, 'OK, now you have had your first kiss. But you just sat there and didn't do anything at all. It was like kissing a piece of raw liver. Now you have to kiss me back.' Which I proceeded to do.

I floated back to the dorm room, feeling things I didn't know existed in the human experience.

I skipped over part of my fourteenth year here because I couldn't wait to tell you the story of my first kiss, but now I have to tell you about perhaps the most important event in my life regarding my profession as an entertainer.

We moved to Corsicana, Texas, in 1980, and while I was as indifferent to moving as I had been the past ten times, I had no idea how it would influence my life forever.

My parents knew how much we loved Mesquite Christian Academy, so they tried to keep us in that school, and for the first semester of school even after we moved, we drove back and forth the hour and fifteen minutes twice a day, but, as always, we ended up moving to another school. We attended several, in fact, over the next few years.

But something happened in 1981 that made all of the pain of continuously changing schools and never being able to keep any friends for more than a few months, not hurt nearly as badly.

Somehow I had discovered about an audition for a review that was to be put on by the city of Corsicana and I got my parents to allow me to audition.

Corsicana was an interesting place, full of a cliquish sensibility, and it was very difficult for any new family to fit into a place where so many families had lived for generations. I think maybe my parents thought it might be a good way for us to fit in a little better, but this is just a guess. Regardless of why they allowed it, I was able to do the audition.

I sang a song and did a little routine with Josh, then did my phone routine where I talked to myself on the phone, providing both my own voice and the far-away sound of the other voice I was talking to.

I was a hit. Years later I was told by one of the Fab Five (I'll explain who they are in a minute) that they met later that night and discussed my audition, where one of them said, 'That was a cute routine, but who was he talking to on the phone?' to which they all laughed and explained that it had all been me. They also agreed that I had more talent than anyone they had ever seen and they determined to use me as much as they could in anything they put together in the future. Now let's go back to who the Fab Five were.

In Corsicana there was a group of five people who were some of the most brilliant entertainment minds you could ever find. Even though the city only had about 25,000 people in it, these five were simply dazzling in their understanding and ability to put a community concert together.

I still feel this way all these years later, and one of the great disappointments of my life is that two of them did not live to see my success on *America's Got Talent*.

The Fab Five were Nancy Roberts, Ann Albritton, John Ron Johnson, Darrell Johnson and Robert Harrod. Each one had a specific talent and brought their own genius to everything they put together, with Nancy Roberts and Ann Albritton arranging the music, John Ron Johnson and Darrell organizing and choreographing the show, and Robert Harrod building the sets and any other props needed. They all wrote the shows together and would spend hours drinking wine and writing material for whatever they happened to be working on at the time.

I never got to go to any of these meetings, but Darrell Johnson and I have become dear friends since, and he told me about them, and we utilized the same techniques (a couple of bottles of wine and friendship, sitting around throwing out ideas) for many of my shows as I became a professional entertainer later on in life.

The first act I did with them was a review about the 1930s, and I got to be Edgar Bergen and Josh got to be Charlie McCarthy. My Edgar and Charlie were perfect, as I was able to recreate their voices impeccably.

The following year was based on the 1940s and I got to be Edgar Bergen and a community leader, Happy Settle, played the part of Mortimer Snerd, a dim-witted country bumpkin character made famous by Mr Bergen. Happy even went so far as to go to an orthodontist and have him make up a set of buck teeth that fitted perfectly. He looked so funny that it took several days before we could rehearse without falling into fits of laughter. He would sit on my knee and move his mouth and I provided his voice, and once again my ability as an impressionist came into the picture as I perfectly replicated Edgar and Mortimer's voices.

But doing these shows had much more of an effect on my life than just getting comfortable on stage and doing impressions.

I was experiencing an independence from the tyranny of my father for the first time. When I was working on those shows my father had no say in anything I did. Well, sort of. He found out one time that in one of the skits we were doing I had to stand close to a beautiful girl named Beth Claxton I had a crush on, so he stormed into the rehearsal and demanded that they move me a few inches from Beth. Of course everyone was stunned at my dad's actions, but they went ahead and moved me a few inches from her. Even though he was always negative about my performances, everyone else I was working with raved about my abilities.

When I would do shows at churches and at school I got compliments, but compliments from show-business people had much more of an impact on me. They knew what they were talking about, didn't they?

My father began to tell me that I wasn't really good at entertaining, but I was good at fooling people into believing I was good. I bought his denigration hook, line, and sinker.

But even though I felt like a fraud, I was still having a ball, since it was my only time away from the drudgery of cleaning buildings and school work.

I got as involved with the Corsicana Warehouse of Living Arts as I could. I tried out for and got parts in *Oliver* (The Artful Dodger), *The Sound of Music* (Rolf), and others, as I continued to get rave reviews from my peers in the arts and even in newspaper articles, one claiming that my cockney accent in *Oliver* was so good it was hard to believe I was a Texan.

The white rabbit continued to beckon me, but I was less interested in him than ever before because I was receiving praise from every other source but my father. For the first time in my entire young life I was able to ignore that rascally rabbit, if only during the days when I was working with my new friends in the performing community. He would haunt my dreams when I was all alone, but the hope of the next time we would be rehearsing made those nightmares bearable.

My dad sometimes protested that I wasn't using my acting for the ministry, but I would remind him that I had to have training in the theater if I was ever to be a preacher, and he accepted my reasoning and allowed me to continue.

I just remembered a great story to give a good example of my naiveté as a teenager. I was fifteen when I began to itch in my nether regions. I had never heard of jock itch and had no idea what was going on but I was terribly uncomfortable for several days. I knew I couldn't consult my father since he would just accuse me of having sex and catching an STD. I suffered in silence and agony for many days until I could take no more. I had scratched myself raw. I decided that it must be chiggers, a small red bug in the south that burrows under your skin and causes itching and discomfort. I came up with the brilliant idea that isopropyl rubbing alcohol would kill the chiggers, so I went into the bathroom and doused a cotton ball with the alcohol. I applied it to the raw, inflamed area and waited. At first it wasn't too bad. It stung a little, but as the seconds ticked by the pain became blinding. I fell to the floor on my knees and everything went red. I had no idea such pain could even be part of the human experience. It lasted for several minutes as I writhed around in agony the entire time. When I could finally stand up, I left the bathroom and confided to Jep what I had endured, and he laughed so hard he couldn't talk for a few minutes, then, through his laughter and tears, explained about jock itch and how all I needed was a cream I could purchase at the pharmacy. So there you are, you now know one of the most embarrassing and painful experiences in my life, but let's get back to the narrative

For several years, I continued to act in as many shows as I could, plus work with the family business *and* go to school. I didn't experience the cliquish mentality that some go through in their high school years, mainly because the schools we went to had a total of about sixty to seventy kids. When I graduated I was valedictorian, but it was in a class of seven—so it was no great honor.

We kept changing from school to school until my senior year when Corsicana Christian Academy was created, and I went to that school for my entire senior year.

I would go to see the Corsicana High School stage productions and I'd yearn to be part of them, sometimes crying myself to sleep because I still felt so lonely and longing to be part of so much that I was missing.

I tried as hard as I could to have a drama club which I, myself, organized at my school. I tried to be a director but I don't have what it takes to direct. I wanted to act, to be the guy getting all the attention, all the glory. I got none at home so I craved it from my peers and colleagues.

The white rabbit beckoned, but I was able to ignore him as long as I was being praised by everyone else. I was haunted by the white rabbit at night lying in bed, though. He was still there no matter how much praise I got. He still haunted my dreams but I was able to forget him in my pursuit of admiration in my daily life. Surely if everyone else saw how talented I was my dad would have to admit it, wouldn't he? I would close my eyes and imagine the white rabbit in my hands, mine forever; the pursuit finally finished and my father admitting that his son was talented and worthwhile.

We had started to attend a new church that boasted of its Biblical literalism, and its members were all very affluent and rich, except for us. It was one of the only times I ever felt like a true outsider even at my church. I now had only one place I felt I belonged and was accepted, and that was on stage.

The church treated us like a ministry, rather than a part of the congregation, and I resented the feeling. We *were* janitors, sure, but I didn't feel any less important because we didn't have a huge house and a swimming pool. Some of the kids always wore designer clothes and were part of the cool crowd at the local high school. We were never treated poorly but we were always treated as a sub-class. This may surprise some of the members of the congregation if they read this, I'm just telling it like it is.

Jep seemed to fit in much better because half of the members had ranches and would use the kids in the church to work on the ranch. It was right up Jep's alley. He loved getting out in the sun and working on the ranch until his hands bled. I, on the other hand, hated it. I tried it once and gave up after a couple of hours. It made me miserable.

I had decided early on that my forte would definitely be in the arts. I had no problem spending countless hours memorizing a play and working until the early morning hours, making sure the show was ready to perform, but get me out on a ranch and it was simply torture. Because of this I was even more spurned by the church members. I was the only kid who refused to work slave labor for less than minimum wage at their ranches so I *must* be lazy.

We were still working just as hard at the family business, but I got away to work with my new-found friends as often as I could.

Debi didn't fit in any more than I did, so we became very close during those years. When our folks dropped us off at a building to clean it, we would try to have as much fun and laugh as much as we could to keep the drudgery away.

Something else began to happen that I had no idea about, but it became crucial to my career. The invention of the Walkman allowed us to listen to our own personalized music mixes as we worked, and I'd sing at the top of my lungs while emptying trash cans and mopping floors.

I was learning to impersonate singers, even though I didn't know it at the time. I would sing along with my favorite Christian singers of the day (Amy Grant, Michael W. Smith, Petra, Daniel Amos, and many others) and work to copy their voices perfectly as I worked.

Once I was singing a Dion DiMucci (he had once been a '50s pop idol and had become a Christian artist) song, and my father heard me and said, 'You sound ridiculous. You're singing the song just like Dion who has spent a lot of time in bars. You've never even seen a bar, much less spent any time in one!'

Despite his criticism, which even at the time sounded ridiculous to me, I practiced singing any song just like any artist I happened to be listening to. I would practice where my father couldn't hear me.

I started to sing the songs of the less rock 'n' roll music at my church. I did Amy Grant and Michael W. Smith and David Meece songs exactly like the records and the church loved it, but they still never treated me like one of them.

I was also using my ability to impersonate singers in my acting career. When playing the part of Rolf in *The Sound of Music* I listened to the record a thousand times and learned to impersonate the guy who played the part in the movie perfectly. Everyone raved except my father, who told me that I wasn't really a good singer but I was excellent at convincing everyone into *thinking* I could sing. I believed him, and wondered how long I could keep fooling people, and I determined to try as long as I could until they figured out the truth.

My sister was as much of an outcast as I was, so I made sure she got involved with the Warehouse Living Arts Center too. We would mow lawns and do odd jobs for anyone we could with the little time we had available, to pay for the cost of joining. We had wonderful times together doing all of that. We grew closer through the rough times at home and by working together outside.

When I turned seventeen I auditioned for, and got the part of, Huckleberry Finn in a production of *The Adventures of Tom Sawyer* that was to be flown over to England to be performed there. I was ecstatic, and I worked for an entire year to raise as much money as I could to spend on the trip. I have no idea why my overbearing father allowed such a trip, but for some reason he did and it really gave me something to look forward to for a whole year.

I got a job as a waiter in a local steakhouse and quickly broke all the records they had for the amount of tips collected.

I would use my ventriloquism as part of my job waiting tables and would have voices crying out from coffee cups and steaks as I delivered the food.

When people came to the steakhouse, they would ask for me to be their waiter because they knew they were going to get a free show as well, and the tips piled up. I was hated by the rest of the wait staff, and they teased me and ridiculed me mercilessly. It got so bad the manager had to make a new rule that customers were not allowed to ask for a specific waiter because the other workers weren't getting any tables to wait on.

I still have some of my former customers come up to me to this day and tell me how much they loved me as a waiter and how funny and clever I was. I did enjoy it, but it made me ever more determined to be a success as an entertainer. I didn't want to be waiting tables; I wanted to be performing on stage.

I finally found a best friend, Mark Erwin, at the Warehouse Living Arts Center, and for that whole year we were inseparable. We were to be going to England together and we spent almost all of our free time talking about how great it would be, and it really was one of the best years of my life. I was less alone, and was so busy I had no time to even think about the loneliness that gnawed at my insides.

During the Christmas season that year we were raising money for the trip with the rest of the cast, and we would go to rich people's Christmas parties and sing carols and do pieces from *Tom Sawyer* for the entertainment of their guests.

I had never before been inside houses like that, and longed to one day be able to buy a house so lovely and spacious. In those days I might as well have desired to have lunch on the moon as to own such a home.

My father was always telling us that God wanted everyone to live simple lives and not to want anything better in life than food and shelter no matter how modest. His attitude suited his laziness perfectly. Why work to have nice things? God doesn't want you to have nice things anyway!

We were lower middle-class janitors, and that was that. We weren't poor, but even though our church-going peers all had the newest and best designer clothes and lived in huge houses with trampolines and swimming pools, we lived in a modest little house in the country and wore generic cheap stuff from Kmart and Sears. It was just the way things were, but I longed for more.

Corsicana was very rural and I was a city guy. I missed the big city and wanted to live where all the action was. By action I mean the big movie theaters. My main love at the time was going to movies. I would get lost in the movies and dream of the day I would be a movie star myself. As I daydreamed I would think of how all of those girls who wouldn't give me the time of day would regret ignoring me when they saw me up on that huge screen!

Corsicana was the first place in Texas to drill for oil so there was a lot of oil money in the city, but there were many more people just like us, barely getting by. My sense of isolation was intensified by my longing to be accepted by those who were rich, while at the same time I was not even accepted by the others in my own working class. We were new and most of them had been in the area for many years. I wanted so much to be the one giving the money to the troupe going to England and not the one asking for help getting there, but again, I had about as much chance of being able to fund the trip as being able to fly.

The trip to England was everything I had dreamed it would be, but something happened to me that was quite unexpected. For the first time in my life I felt truly free from the ever-present and watchful eye of my father. A whole ocean separated us and I knew he couldn't possibly show up and ruin my trip.

When I was fifteen I had gone to one of the competitions for my school that was a few hours' drive from my home. A beautiful young lady had asked me to dinner one night and I had to refuse her invitation because I was terrified my parents would drive there to make sure I wasn't doing anything they disapproved of. I spent the evening sitting next to a creek, aching from the loneliness I felt as I thought of her eating dinner with someone else.

But this time I knew there was no way they could come and spy on me.

As a result I was, for the first time in my life, truly free to express myself in any way I chose, and I did. I went nuts, chattering on and on, laughing and joking and probably driving everyone around me crazy, but I didn't care.

A few months ago I was talking with one of the adults who went on that trip and told them I must have been a terror, but they assured me that as everyone knew the kind of oppression I suffered at the hands of my tyrannical father, they were delighted to see me so happy, if not just a little annoyed at my antics.

I met a lovely girl named Claire and, as I had done numerous times before (Julie, Kim, Rita, Sally and all the others) promptly fell in love. We spent as much time as we could with one another, with Mark Erwin and my room-mate, Jerry Ferrell, alongside as well.

I had never experienced such joy and freedom before, and the prospect of it ending was almost too much to bear. Ten days can seem like such a long time to a kid, but it does end, just like everything else in life. I think when I get to heaven it will be much as it was during those ten days. I was blissfully unaware that I had a controlling father back home waiting for me, the drudgery of more cleaning of buildings, and more of the mundane and lonely life I had led up until that point.

I remember little of the actual show we did. All I can recall is the laughter and friendship I felt with all the kids I met in England, especially Claire. I considered throwing my passport away before I got to the airport and telling the authorities I had lost it. I thought maybe it might buy me a few days more, but sanity prevailed and I didn't do it.

As I walked toward the plane to leave, Claire came up and kissed me hard. I think maybe I'll always have a little bit of a crush on her for doing that. I said goodbye and boarded the plane back to America.

As the plane lifted its wheels, I burst into a fit of weeping, realizing with a sudden rush that the freedom I had felt during the fleeting moments in England were rapidly coming to an end and I would soon be back under tyranny and in misery.

Those who came with me felt my pain and sympathized. It was obvious to everyone I knew that I had an overbearing father and I was unhappy at home, but they were as helpless as I to help in any way.

I had taken several hundred pictures of my trip to England, of Claire and all my new friends, but as he had done many times before in my life, my father decided that I spent too much time looking at them and burned them all. I have nothing but memories left of the most wonderful time of my life.

One of the things that had kept me sane during those years was fantasy books. As we were not allowed any non-Christian materials in our house I had come to depend on Christian fantasy like C.S. Lewis' *Chronicles of Narnia* and books by Stephen Lawhead and John White. These books were an immense source of comfort to me as I would hide under the covers late at night with a flashlight and be transported to strange and unknown locations, where I pretended to be the hero who saved the land from peril and, of course, got the girl in the end.

I was traveling to these fantasy worlds constantly, whether through those books, or on stage pretending to be someone else entirely and getting applause for my troubles.

One day my father told me that I had become obsessed with my fantasy books, so he took them away from me and threw them in a dumpster somewhere in the city.

I truly felt that I could not live without that source of escape, so Debi and I spent the entire next day combing every dumpster in the city until we found my precious books. We climbed into one dumpster after another and sorted through the garbage until at last we found the stack of precious books. I'm sure I looked strange to anyone who might have seen me, as well as reeking of stale garbage by the time I finished, but my desperation at the thought of losing those books was so intense I cared nothing for what anyone else might think, I only knew I had to have them. I collected them and hid them in my room, trying to find a place they could never be found, and would only read them in the dark of night, panicking and hiding them quickly if I ever heard even the slightest noise outside my door.

I find it hilarious when I look back and realize that while most of my teen friends were probably hiding *Playboy* magazines from their folks, I was hiding a collection of Christian fantasy novels, but there it was.

Comic books were also not allowed in our house, so I also had a number of *Spiderman* and *The Incredible Hulk* comics under my mattress. Once when I was fifteen my mother cleaned our room and found my comic book stash and turned me in to my father.

He called my school and told me that he had found my comic books and I would be punished when I got home. I was so terrified that I ran away from the school, determined to get a ride on an eighteen-wheeler and start a whole new life somewhere. I was only fifteen, and once again sanity prevailed. I called home and had my parents pick me up and I dealt with the consequences, which, as I recall, were not as bad as I thought. The comic books were, of course, destroyed, but I don't think I even got a spanking for that one.

My parents did, however, send me to a psychiatrist, who told me after several sessions that I held my dad too high up on a pedestal and really should realize that he was, after all, human, and not the end-all be-all that I had built him up to be in my head.

I was furious! My father was a man of God and just wanted the best for me, I argued, and after I told my dad what the psychiatrist had said, he promptly took me out of the sessions and I never went back.

Only one other time did I run away from home; or rather I was kicked out of the house.

I was seventeen, and my brother had got into an argument with my dad in the car over something silly and my father had stopped the car and kicked him out of it, telling him that he wasn't welcome in our family any more.

As I watched my brother walking away from the car my dad continued to scream at me. I guess he must have asked me a question, but I had become so good at zoning my father out when he would scream and yell for what seemed like eternity, I didn't hear what he had said.

He was furious and said, 'Well, if you are going to take his side you aren't welcome in this family either.' He stopped the van, came around to my door, opened it up, grabbed me by the collar, and threw me to the ground. He then proceeded to get our moped out of the van, threw it on top of me, screaming, 'Here! Now you can just get the hell out of here!' He got in the van and floored it, throwing dust and gravel over me as the wheels spun and he drove away.

My first emotion was fear. I had no idea where to go or what I would do. In a panic I drove the moped to my friend Darrell Johnson's house and told him what had happened.

He accepted me into his home and assured me that I would always have a place to stay and that I was welcome to live with him for as long as I needed, even if it was for the whole school year.

I was to be a senior and the thought of going to the public school for the year made me happier than anything that had happened to me in my entire life so far. I was finally free of my rigid home life and I was ready to party. I planned on going out that night to the local video game arcade, hopefully to meet girls.

Before I left, one of the most important moments of my life happened. I don't think even Darrell knows how much that moment meant to me, and I'm sure as he reads this it will surprise him, but he asked me to sit down at the table because he wanted to talk to me.

As far as girls and sex were concerned, all I knew from my parents was that God would strike me down if I ever touched a girl inappropriately if she wasn't my wife. I was terrified of sex and had been told many times that if I ever did sin with a girl I could never have a happy marriage, and God would abandon me.

As Darrell began to talk, I interrupted him. 'I know, I know, if I have sex before marriage I'll ruin my life,' I hastily told him, anxious to be out on my bike.

'Well, that's not exactly true,' he told me, and proceeded to explain in a frank and honest fashion that with relationships with girls comes responsibility, and that may include undesirable consequences. 'If you are not ready to be a father, think hard about what you do. Nothing may happen, but on the other hand, anything *could* happen. Just think about it.'

Now this may seem to you to be a very simple and innocuous conversation, but it was the first time anyone had just simply been honest with me about girls. Sex wasn't the worst thing in the world, just try to be handle myself responsibly.

And that is exactly what I did. I did go to the arcade that night, but much more in control of my emotions and I didn't do anything I might regret later, simply because my friend had been honest and open with me. Thanks for that, Darrell.

I stayed with Darrell and his wonderful family for a week (painting his game room as payment for lodging) before patching things up with my family.

I then went back into the darkness, giving up all the hopes and dreams of being part of the high school drama club, and all of the other wonderful things I hoped for my senior year at Corsicana High School, and moved back into the oppression.

However, my senior year wasn't as terrible as I had envisioned. I had a lot of fun with several of my new friends and actually got to stay in the same school for the entire year. I made a great friend in Chris Turner, whose parents owned the local Christian bookstore. Mark Erwin, Chris, Debi and I became inseparable and would spend all of our free time (I didn't have a lot of it, but some) together listening to Weird Al and Monty Python records. My father wouldn't have approved but what he didn't know wouldn't hurt him.

Chris Turner and I dreamed of being a famous Christian comedy duo. We eagerly wrote several Christian comedy routines and fantasized about the day we could afford to actually record them. We never got the chance to do it, but we did have a lot of fun dreaming about it.

We would go regularly to Christian rock concerts and would sometimes dress in funny clothes to try to draw attention to ourselves. I would watch the performers and ache inside to do what they did. How I wanted to be an entertainer, especially with a live audience where I could hear the cheers and feel the excitement.

Countless times my brother, sister, and Chris would go to the concerts, and then pizza afterwards, excitedly discussing the show.

I had begun to do little concerts for my friends and family, utilizing an amazing new invention called a Vocal Eliminator, which would take the lead vocals out of a song, allowing me to sing pretty much anything I wanted. I was able to impersonate any vocal I came across and I put on some great concerts at school, church, and even the local community college student union.

I would sing a few songs, then bring out Josh and do a comedy routine, then do more music, followed by another puppet, and so on.

People loved my shows and would rave on and on about them to me, much to my delight.

I was still not too popular with the girls, and most of the ones I developed crushes on had no interest in me at all. I was the guy every parent wanted their daughter to date, but none of the girls wanted.

One of these girls was Julie, a lovely young lady on the Corsicana High School drill team. We lived out in the country and our road passed by her house. I eagerly searched for her every time I was driving home, longing for just a glimpse of her walking her dog. I only saw her a few times but it was always a thrill to actually see her. I finally got up the courage to call her up. I looked up her phone number (in a phone book—this was years before the Internet!) I could hear the ringing sound in the receiver. 'Hello?' the angelic voice said on the other end of the receiver. I took a deep breath.

'May I speak to Julie?' I asked nervously.

'This is her,' she answered sweetly.

I started babbling on about something I can't remember, mentioned a book, and it was all over. I have no idea what I said but later someone told me that she thought I was weird. I had panicked and couldn't think of anything to say to her except to babble on about one of my favorite Christian fantasy books. I don't recommend it to any of you young people reading this. Hot teenage girls on the drill team don't care about Christian fantasy. Who knew?

My self image was fast waning, and I was spiraling down into someone who thought of himself as worthless and unattractive. I don't think it helped that my father was constantly telling me that I wasn't very good-looking and that it would be a struggle to ever get accepted as an entertainer. I still have a very hard time with my looks to this day. No matter how much Melinda and Debi tell me I'm a decent-looking guy I can't accept it as fact. (I mean, your wife and sister are supposed to say stuff like that, aren't they?)

On my eighteenth birthday my friends from the Warehouse Living Arts Center got together to give me a party, organized by Darrell Johnson and my mom, and they did a *This Is Your Life*-themed party. It was wonderful!

All of my friends got up and told stories about the shows I had done, and then to end the party I was given a large box. I opened it and found a real, honest-to-goodness professional ventriloquist figure staring up at me.

My mother (bless her!) had called up a professional vent figure carver (Craig Lovik) and had explained to him that I wanted to be a pro but could not afford a real professional figure. He said that he had one in his office that he wasn't quite happy with and he would gladly sell it to her for a fraction of the cost. For three years she had saved and sent Mr Lovik money until she had enough to buy him, and here he was, my first real professional ventriloquist figure.

I don't think I ever saw anything more beautiful in my entire life.

I picked him up gingerly and did a little routine for my guests, tears welling up in my eyes, trying hard to manage my emotions as I felt the smooth controls and saw the flawless action of the slotted mouth and moving eyes, eyebrows and eyelids.

I will never forget that wonderful moment, and to this day he is my most prized possession. He was to become Walter T. Airdale, country music legend and yodeler, after several other incarnations including a surfer with a Mohawk and a heavy-metal singer with leather and long hair.

I now knew I would be able to fulfill my dreams and was on the road to doing it.

After the long, satisfying day, I packed my new character back into his box and went home and my father said to me, 'That skit you did today was terrible. I sure hope you don't waste all the money your mother spent with crap like that.'

But as I lay in bed, delirious from all the wonderful attention and thinking of my new partner, even those harsh words couldn't diminish my excitement. I was going to do it! I was going to be a famous ventriloquist!

And all those girls who had rejected me would one day say to themselves, 'What did I do? I could've dated Terry Fator and I blew it!'

I smiled as I drifted off to sleep. *They'll see. I can do it. I know I can...*

Chapter 5

Growing Up

Was it really as bad as all that? I read over the chapter I just wrote and wondered if I was remembering it correctly—so I sent it to my brother Jep for his reaction.

Jep called me the next day and said he cried when he read the last chapter and that I had really glossed over the reality of the situation. It was, in fact, much worse, and I had left out a lot of the really difficult stuff. I replied that I didn't want people to feel too despondent after they read my book, so I would leave it as written. He laughed and agreed, but at least he confirmed that I'm on the right track.

My real goal here is for you, the reader, to feel the emotion I felt as I went through my life, and according to Jep I'm doing well so far so we'll just keep going.

If our high school years are the best years of our lives, then I guess that a lot of times we are not motivated to make the future as bright as possible—so maybe that explains why so many successful people have had difficult childhoods. At least that's my theory.

Everything I described to you is exactly how I felt, but darker times were ahead. As I got into my senior year of high school, Jep went away to college to Montana Wilderness

Bible College and experienced for a whole year the ecstasy of freedom I had tasted, away from my father's watchful eye.

For the first time in his life he got to listen to the music he wanted (including—gasp—non-Christian rock music!) and date girls—one in particular, Pam Hansen, who was to become his wife.

I loved not having to share a room for the first time ever, and my year at Corsicana Christian Academy was not a bad one. My sister went to the same school, even though she was three years younger; and after cleaning the school as tuition payment, many days we would walk the three miles to the Warehouse Living Arts Center to rehearse a play we were in, and those days were always a joy.

Our parents would pick us up after rehearsal and take us to whatever building we had to clean for the night, but even that was OK because we laughed a lot and listened to our music, and really made it a fun time instead of drudgery.

Those were good times because my father had decided he didn't feel like working and stayed home, and we didn't see him very often. The dark cloud that resided over our household didn't travel beyond those walls, so as long as we weren't home it didn't affect us very much. My dad pretty much slept and watched television all the time, so until we got home we didn't have to deal with him.

I still recall vividly the feeling that no matter how happy we were or how much fun we had had during the day, as soon as we got home we knew it would all end, and we would probably get screamed at for something; because of the dark cloud over our house, we dreaded going there.

It was a daily routine: school, rehearsal for a play, cleaning a building, and home to get into trouble. However, in spite of the darkness of those times, one of the great life lessons we all learned during those times was that 'This, too shall pass.'

There were times when we literally had to work for thirty-six to sixty straight hours without rest or sleep, often to strip and wax the floors at Kmart in Corsicana.

Those days were misery beyond what a normal American child can imagine. We would be mopping and mopping and after about thirty, forty and more hours I would literally think to myself, *I have died and gone to hell and this is the punishment for my sins. This will never end; I'll just have to do this for all of eternity.*

But inevitably it would end and I would finally be snug in my bed afterwards, thinking as I drifted off to sleep, *It really is over. I'm done and now I can sleep!*

To this day I use those feelings to help my sister Debi out when she has a really bad day.

At sixteen years old, Debi began to notice that her joints were hurting, and it was difficult for her to carry around the five-gallon buckets of water and stripping fluid we used in our business. When she complained, my father accused her of being lazy and trying to get out of work, so would add even more chores to her load.

One day when she was eighteen, she was in so much pain she couldn't even get out of bed, and no amount of screaming and belittling from my father could change it, so my mom took her to the doctor where she was diagnosed with advanced rheumatoid arthritis.

They had never seen such an advanced case of the disease in so young a person. I think it progressed so rapidly because of the stress induced by my dad's increasing irrationality and his religious demands on us.

At one point, when Debi had been sixteen, he thought she had been dating a boy behind his back (it wasn't true, but he thought she was) so he grabbed her by the hand and turned on our gas stove and force her hand over the flame, holding it and burning her so she could feel what hell was like if she continued to disobey him.

I had heard her screams, but felt powerless to help because I knew I had hell to look forward to also if I defied my father—so I hid in my room and wept as I heard her struggling to get away from him.

One thing he made clear to all of us from the time we were very young children was that God would not tolerate any disobedience of our dad at any point in our lives. To lose my dad's blessing was to lose God's blessing, and since I so desperately wanted God to bless me, I felt I had to always make sure my father approved of my life.

There was no end to this rule, and I can't tell you how often I wished my dad would die so I could be free of the curse. I'm ashamed to admit it, but I honestly thought it was the only way to be free of that requirement.

Anyway, even now when Debi calls me and tells me she is having a really rough day and doesn't know how much more she can take, I tell her that she's just stripping and waxing the floors at Kmart, and she laughs and agrees and it helps get her through the rough patch.

Later on I learned how to do hypnosis for Debi because I heard that it could help with pain. To this day she can call me whenever she is having trouble and I do a session for her over the phone with fantastic results.

I had told you my brother went off to college, and during that year life at the Fator household was pretty normal. In the country in Corsicana, Texas, we city folk tried to pretend we were country folk, and we even got a few chickens and a rooster. The only rooster we had was a little slow, but affectionate, and we called him 'George the retarded rooster'. He would peck at our feet to get us to show him attention and we thought it was quite funny.

Once during a terrible freeze we went outside the next day and found that all of our chickens (and George) had roosted in the trees and were still there, frozen solid. We actually had a chicken coop, but had no idea how to get them to use it. (I told you, we had lived in the city most of our lives!)

As sad as it was to see our chickens frozen we did laugh about it quite a bit, but then a miracle happened. As the sun came out and it got a little warmer all of the chickens (and George) began to stir, and it turned out that they weren't dead after all. George never fully recovered however; his crown wilted and turned black and he was never the same. He would no longer peck us for attention, but would chase us in a rage as though somehow it was our fault he was frozen to the tree (I think I would have reacted the same way if it had happened to me), clucking and roosting quite animatedly.

It got so bad we had to check around and make sure he wasn't near the car when we got home. If he was, we made a mad dash into the house so he wouldn't attack us. I know we probably could just have got rid of him, but I think we all felt a little guilty about him freezing and all, so we tolerated him. Once Debi had a birthday party and we invited some girls over for it (I can't really call them friends since we all felt they looked down on Debi and us for our position in life as janitors), and I had the position of the watch. I would wait until a guest's car pulled up, then lure George away and have him chase me as the girl made a clean getaway to where the party was being held, in a little clearing in the woods (we had five acres of land we had purchased from my grandmother).

My grandmother was not nearly as tolerant of George's antics as we were, however, and on one of her visits to us, George mysteriously disappeared, but we did have a delicious fried chicken dinner that night. I wonder whatever happened to old George...

Life as a city boy in a country world went on and we survived (barely) through the hottest summer in Texas history, with more than a full month straight of one hundred degree-plus temperatures.

The days of cleaning buildings raced by, day after day, and we were just thankful that the buildings we cleaned were air-conditioned.

Jep came home during the Christmas holidays and announced that he had fallen in love, and we were all so happy for him.

Everyone except, guess who? Our father. He screamed and railed about how my brother gets a little freedom and goes out and ruins his life. Jep protested and told him that Pam was a wonderful girl and that she made him happy.

My father was incensed and said that he had a plan for our lives; he had dedicated us all to God's service, and it didn't include spouses. Jep told him it was too late and he was in love and would probably marry Pam. My dad was furious and went into the house and grabbed a rifle we had there, informing us that he would rather see us dead than see us not follow his plan for us.

We wrestled the gun out of his hands and I got every gun we had in the house and ran. I ran for miles, crying and wondering what we were going to do. I had feared my father for most of my life, but for the first time I wasn't just scared of him, I was terrified. He obviously had plans for us that didn't include our approval or consent, and I didn't know what to do.

I learned later that he had grabbed my brother by the neck and had tried to choke him, with my mother and sister hitting him with shoes or whatever they could find, until he let Jep go.

Later my father told us he just wanted to scare us and never intended to kill us—but I saw the look in his eyes and I'll never buy his story. He was completely insane that day and I know he would have been capable of anything if we hadn't stopped him.

I have no memory how all of this was resolved, but I was forever scarred and was deathly afraid of my dad from that moment on. I think all of us were.

Jep did end up marrying Pam and she became one of the true delights of our lives from the time she and Jep got together. Later they had a daughter and she was the greatest joy to all of us, my wife and Debi included. We doted on her and spoiled her, since she was the only kid around. For years, Christmas was a spectacular event that revolved around Alyssa, Jep and Pam's daughter and my niece. I still spoil her. Since she has been with us she has been such an important part of my sanity.

We would torment her with practical jokes as she grew, all in good humor, but I think some of them may have emotionally scarred her. Once when she was around six we told her that there was going to be a meteor shower that night. It was true, but what wasn't true was what we had told her about children watching it. We explained that kids had to wear protection in order to see the meteors without hurting their eyes, so we proceeded to find any and everything we could in the tour bus (we had a band and were travelling around in a bus) for her to wear. We wrapped her head up in tin foil with tiny holes poked for her to see and breathe, placed a scarf around her head, made her wear mittens and about three coats, and put sunglasses on her. She looked like a baked Mr. Potato Head. I can still recall how funny it was to see her like that, but also how excited she was at the prospect of seeing the meteor shower, so she sat on the couch in the living area of the bus, bouncing up and down excitedly in her ridiculous attire. She didn't care what she looked like as long as she got to see it. We could finally take no more and we burst out laughing and told her we were just kidding, unwrapped her and let her go out normally to watch it.

Another time Alyssa had crawled under some bleachers and was playing in a stack of old hay with a couple of little kids she met, and she got lice. She had to have her hair shampooed with special solution, and then we all went out to eat at a restaurant. Debi had just bought a little harness for her cat, but we told Alyssa that we had bought it for her and she had to wear it until the lice was gone. We put it on her head and pretended to be walking into the restaurant when she started to cry. We felt terrible about her crying, so we all hugged her and told her we were just joking.

All of our little practical jokes were very good-natured and never cruel or mean, but I think Alyssa has a hard time trusting anything anyone tells her because we were always joking about stuff with her.

She took the jokes with good humor and even though she occasionally cried, she would always laugh with us once she knew we were kidding her.

Anyway, all that happened much later in life, but I was just thinking about her and how much fun we had with her and got sidetracked. Let's get back to the time-line again.

During my senior year in high school I became friends with Russell Kelly. I have a hard time calling him an 'African American' because the term had not even been invented then, and he was part of the only black family at Believer's Bible Church. Russell and I became very close friends, I think because he felt that they were part of the other church members' 'ministry' like we did (they were, like us, lower middle class in a world of upper-class churchgoers).

Like Chris Turner, Russell and I wanted to be a comedy team, and we used to make comic radio shows that were never broadcast. I still have them on cassette tape. When we were in our senior year in high school we were counselors at the Believer's Bible Church vacation Bible school and we used the opportunity to write several original comedy routines. During the final evening of vacation Bible school Russell and I had written a comedy routine based on one of the stories the children had learned about a missionary to one of the African countries.

Much to the shock and dismay of the wealthy prim and proper church attendees Russell dressed in African garb (shirtless!) and we shocked the audience with our strange brand of comedic takes on the missionary's life. For example, at one point as I was teaching the native (Russell) how to read I held up a picture of an apple and said, 'A is for apple' to which Russell started to dance around and sing 'J is for jacks, cinnamon toasty Apple Jacks!'

At another point one of the missionaries had been beheaded. Russell took a machete to Josh (my ventriloquist dummy) and pretended to cut his head off and I held up just the head of Josh while he told Russell that he forgave him for killing him. I know it was pretty bizarre stuff but Russell and I thought it was all very funny and I think it was even funnier when we saw the shocked expressions of those who had treated us as their 'ministry'. The church members sat in stunned silence and didn't know what to say after we finished.

Russell was an amazing singer as well and I always loved to hear him sing. We talked about one day starting a vocal group but it never got off the ground.

I lost contact with Russell and have not seen him in several years. Russell's mother passed away during the time I knew him and I think my friendship meant a lot to him at the time. I know he certainly meant an enormous amount to me and I will always think fondly of the times I had with him. I would love to see Russell again sometime and I hope his life has taken him to wonderful places.

Whatever gripes I have about my father (and I have many) one thing I will always be thankful for is the fact that he taught us three children from our earliest memories that God loves all humanity and race should never be an issue. I can honestly say that I never heard him utter a racist remark and as a result I do not judge anyone based on their race. I know Jep and Debi feel the same way.

After high school graduation I was accepted to Liberty Baptist College, which my dad approved of, since they kept strict tabs on students, and the chances of me actually developing free thought were remote. At least that was his theory, but I had learned to fool my dad by that time. I had my own thoughts and feelings but kept them locked up tight so no-one knew how I really felt, and therefore I couldn't get into trouble for actually developing my own opinions.

Unfortunately Liberty Baptist College wasn't prepared for me, and I think to this day they still haven't recovered.

They had so many ridiculous rules that I hated, and while I would obey the letter of the law, I would find every way possible to bend the rules to accommodate my free spirit.

For example, we had to wear ties all the time. Get up to go to breakfast? Wear a tie. Go to the Students' Lounge to play a video game? Tie. I thought it was idiotic that there was no place you could go on campus without wearing a tie. You could never feel relaxed, or at home.

In spite of the fact that this was the early '80s and very thin ties were the style, I went to Goodwill and bought out every gigantic flowery tie from the early '70s they had, and wore those gaudy things every single day to show that I had no problem wearing ties, but that I would do it on my own terms.

'College for a Weekend' was coming up, and that meant that high school students would be arriving from all over the world to see if they liked the college.

I wanted to be sure that these new prospects understood they would have to wear ties, so I put on every single colorful and flowery I owned (over eighty of them), hanging them from my arms and legs, and walked around every day with ties hanging off me. When I received the obvious stares from everyone around, I explained that I wanted to be sure these new students knew that ties were required. I was told by the authorities that I had to take them off and wear only one tie at a time, but I replied that if they could find it in the rule book and show it to me, I would gladly consent. They couldn't, so I wore all of the ties the whole weekend. I think to this day they have a rule that states only one tie should be worn at a time. At least that's what someone told me. I became a hero to many of the students and an enemy to the more straight-laced of the group.

I did this sort of thing regularly. I hated being forced to go to chapel every morning at the crack of dawn, so I would hide under my bed and read comic books, which, thankfully, I didn't have to hide under my mattress.

Casper, *Richie Rich*, and *Spiderman* as well as (gasp!) non-Christian fantasy novels were my constant companions during those chapel mornings, at least until the RAs (Resident

Assistants) figured out my tricks and began checking under my bed when they did the room checks to make sure everyone was at chapel.

I was actually suspended both semesters when I was at school for skipping chapel.

I just wanted to be free to go to church and chapel when *I* wanted, and not be forced to, but this was my dad's plan all along, to keep me under authority and not allow me to think for and act for myself.

It wasn't a bad year, all said. I did sneak off campus regularly with friends (we were also not allowed off campus without permission, but I did anyway). Hardy's Steak and Egg Biscuits were a staple of college life as we would sneak off campus at 2am to feed our habit. Do you see now why I didn't want to get up at the crack of dawn to go to chapel? I was still digesting my late-night biscuit when it was time for chapel!

I never got involved in drugs or alcohol abuse and never had a desire to, but I still had to feed the rebel in me, and he craved steak and egg biscuits!

My brother Jep was there as well and we spent a lot of time together, and I'll never forget the night all the guys in our dorm were sitting around talking, and the subject of Terry-bashing came around. Jep was infuriated, and informed those saying I would end up a nothing, and in trouble because I didn't follow the rules, that I would make more of my life that all of them put together, and that I had a heart for God that none of them could come close to, and to shut up. I was never more proud in my life than at that moment, and I will always appreciate Jep's words that night.

I had decided that my major would be drama since that was what I loved the most in life—and my drama teacher was Steven Wedan, a man who had a great influence on me, even though he had no idea of it. I had never met anyone like him before. He was a Christian, as it was a Christian college I was attending, but he was much more laid-back than any Christian I had ever known. I had been raised to believe that all Christians had to be very uptight about everything, always looking for evil in everyone and everything, but Mr Wedan didn't do that. He actually seemed to *enjoy* life with a passion I had never experienced.

He taught us all the techniques of acting, most of which were far too advanced for my ADD-addled seventeen-year-old brain, but most of which stayed with me for years to come, and I have been able to utilize those techniques in my career many times since college.

Once again I was on the outside looking in, since the drama department was extremely cliquish, and the only insiders were the ones who had known each other for years, and since I was a freshman I couldn't break through that barrier - but I was OK with it. I fitted in here much better than anywhere else in the school, so it became my refuge.

I even used it to bend the school rules again.

I auditioned for *Fiddler on the Roof* and got a part. It was the first time in my life I had auditioned for a role and not been given the lead, but as I was a lowly freshman, it was to be expected, and I wasn't disappointed; I was ecstatic. I got to be in a college play.

I was so excited and I worked as hard as I could to be the best Mendel the Rabbi's son I could.

I began to grow my hair out (school rules demanded that men's haircuts be extra-short) for the show, and any time I was reprimanded I told them I was growing my hair for a school play and I got away with it. I was so sneaky.

We did the show and it was one of the most enjoyable experiences of my life.

A number of practical jokes were played, such as a scene in which one of the characters raises a glass and shouts 'La Heim!' and drinks what was supposed to be an alcoholic beverage replaced with water (it was a very strict Baptist college after all), but had been substituted with vodka one night as a joke.

The guy downed the vodka (thinking it was water) like he had done every other night, and when the lights blacked out as they were supposed to, the audience heard a gigantic wheeze and coughing, as well as gales of laughter from all of us who had been in on the joke.

As we were preparing for the last show (we ran for three weeks) a friend of mine, Bart Truman, told me that when he looked at Mr Wedan he was going to cross his eyes to test Mr Wedan's concentration. Bart then proceeded to demonstrate what he would do. It looked absolutely hilarious and made me break out into fits of laughter every time he did it.

As the show progressed I got more and more excited to see how Mr Wedan would react to Bart's eye-crossing and when the scene was finally over and Mr Wedan had no reaction whatsoever I was impressed, until I found out that Bart had chickened out and couldn't bring himself to do it. He did, however, look at me and cross his eyes as we were walking in a circle singing *Anatevka*, the saddest song in the whole show, a very somber moment in which the entire village is lamenting the fact that they have to leave their beloved village and start their lives over in a new area.

I immediately burst out laughing but masked it by pretending I was crying. This, in turn, sent almost all of the rest of the cast into fits of giggling and laughing in this intense moment, and all of us were snickering and giggling uncontrollably, pretending we were crying.

After the performance, one particularly uptight guy

I was three when my baby sister was born. Here's me (right) and Jep with our new baby sister!

Ahhh, the summer days of the '70s!

Aren't we cute? Jep was six, I was five, and Debi was two in this lovely photo.

I never minded playing Robin to Jep's Batman.
We were four and five in this picture.

Family photo when I was nine. This was before things got really dark.

Can you pick me out of the crowd? I was ten. I still laugh out loud whenever I see this. I hope the other students have forgiven me!

North Lake Elementary School   1975-76   Richardson, Texas

When I was nine I wrote a love letter to my teacher Miss Timberlake. My penmanship has not improved at all since then!

11-year-old not a dummy

When people ask 11-year-old Terry Fator what he wants to be when he grows up they may not be surprised with his answer: A minister.

And if the sixth-grader at Northlake Elementary School doesn't have a change of heart about the ministry, his congregation, years from now, could be one of the most talked about ones in the city.

Because not every congregation has a pastor who is also a ventriloquist.

"I've been thinking about becoming a minister, but I also like ventriloquism and maybe I could do both," Terry said.

Terry, who first became interested in ventriloquism six months ago after checking out a library book on the subject, has become somewhat of a celebrity around school and the neighborhood.

He and his dummy Josh (short for Joshua) have been in demand to perform at school and community activities.

"My husband and I are thrilled about what Terry is doing," said Mrs. Jep Fator, Terry's mother.

Mrs. Fator said Terry earned the money to purchase his dummy by babysitting.

Terry said his goal is to be famous one day.

Terry Fator and Josh prepare for a sermon.

One of my very first newspaper articles in the *Dallas Morning News*.

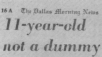

Here's a calendar we shot for the Tom Sawyer play. The guy to my left is Jerry Farrell. I can't remember the name of the girl but I had a crush on her anyway. I think she liked Jerry.

I was ten and doing a show for my uncle and aunt at their house. I love the '70s dress and decor!

Christmas 1974—I got a magic
kit and I loved it!

Me and Freckles getting ready to perform!

Even at 18, I never stopped believing!

My eighteenth birthday when I received my first professional vent figure, who was to become country legend Walter T. Airdale.

This is an early incarnation of Walter T. Airdale. I'm not sure who looks scarier, me or him!

Anything to get attention! I had dressed up like a character from one of Steve Taylor's videos and gone to his concert like this! I'm surprised I ever had any girlfriends at all!

TEXAS the band—sunglasses, long hair and pointing at the camera—we were trying to look cool.

This is a special picture—Melinda and me on our very first vacation together in Paris!

Melinda and me with Nancy Reagan. I was stunned to find out she's a fan of mine! Just how does one process that information?

Me with (from left) Duggie Scott Walker, Julius, and Winston the Impersonating Turtle

berated me for my loss of concentration, screaming at me that I would never be able to be an actor and that I had ruined the whole show.

The rest of the cast who had not been able to control their own laughter came to my defense, and Bart reminded him that we were just in college and we should be having a good time anyway.

When we went out to meet the crowd many of the audience members told us that our sadness and weeping during the song 'Anatevka' was very moving and had made them cry, since it really looked like we were expressing grief, so I guess we were able to really make it look like tears and it was a success after all.

I never saw Bart Truman again, but we had a great time during that play.

I didn't excel at drama since usually when Mr Wedan told us to learn a monologue I would just do a Monty Python skit, complete with the English accent and everything, leading to Mr Wedan banning Monty Python routines from being used in class.

I made it through my one year of college with middling grades, partially because an epidemic of the infectious disease, mononucleosis, hit the campus, and I was a casualty.

I found out I had it during a karate class. We were doing some exercises and I collapsed. Everyone thought I was faking it and they were making fun of me, but I couldn't walk or stand up. Jep came by luckily and found me outside the door on the ground. I had crawled over to the door and had sat, unable to leave. Thankfully Jep saw that I was really sick and helped me get to my room.

I hated that I had gotten the so-called "kissing disease" without the benefits of kissing anyone, but at least I now had a doctor's excuse to not have to get up and go to chapel, and I used it for the rest of the year. It caused me physical problems over the next few years, since I unusually contracted the disease several times in the next decade and ended up with Chronic Fatigue Syndrome. I still have trouble with it, but can control it as long as I take care of myself and don't push too hard, and get plenty of rest.

While at college that year I began to utilize my ability to impersonate singers again. I started to do my favorite impressions for my friends at college.

It was the time of Michael Jackson and *Thriller* and he had just won a ton of Grammys for his work. I loved the album *Thriller*, and as I was not at home my father couldn't tell me I wasn't allowed to have the album, so I had it in my collection.

My friends at college started saying that the only way Michael Jackson could sing like that was if he was on female hormones or had been castrated. I informed them that was ridiculous and I could sing like that if I wanted, so of course, I had to prove it. I actually learned how to impersonate Michael Jackson singing 'Billie Jean', changing the words to represent the fact that we were not allowed to wear blue jeans at Liberty Baptist College. I think the words were something like 'Billie Jean is not my mother, she just an RA who claims that I am the one, wearing jeans, to my class, in the school...' or something silly like that, but it was a huge hit, and I used to go from dorm to dorm and sing the songs in Michael Jackson's voice, and would take up a collection from the students to pay for my steak and egg biscuit habit.

I even entered a college version of the *Dating Game* for the boys' dorm in which the winner won a double date with the winner of the girls' version of the game. I went on as Michael Jackson, doing the high-pitched voice and infusing the 'Whoo-Hoo's' and songs from his album. The girl was so intrigued to see what I really looked like that she chose me, and was mortified to find out she would be going out with the guy who wore all those ties during College for a Weekend. It wasn't a successful date and she thought I was very weird, which I guess I was, now that I think of it. What the heck did she expect, the real Michael Jackson? Sheesh!

I got out of college and, as usual, had lost all of my friends from high school and college, in moving on to my new experiences. I would love to find old friends like Mark Erwin again and talk over old times, but have had no luck finding him on the internet. I hope to one day hear from him again.

I have run into Chris Turner a few times but we have never had the opportunity to reminisce, and I would love to do that as well.

Things in my life were set to take an interesting turn and I was about to really learn how to be an entertainer—so there was no time to look back now. Full speed ahead into the next chapter of my life!

Chapter 6
Band Aid

I had now learnt to manipulate my dad, and was easily able to convince him that anything I did to forward my career was actually part of my training for the ministry.

After college I came back home (I had to if I wanted God to bless me—my father said so) and went back to work with the family. We had expanded our janitorial business to include getting houses and apartments ready to sell and rent, so we would literally go in and remodel the entire house.

It was the most grueling work we ever did and we put in many hours every single day. I spent much of that time singing to the radio and practicing my ventriloquism. I'd be painting walls, and going over my ABCs without moving my lips for hours on end.

I longed to entertain, but there seemed no way to break into the field, until one day we heard about a Christian organization that performed at high schools and middle schools around the country, providing a drug-and-alcohol awareness program for teens.

It turned out they needed a singer in one of their many touring bands, and I got the job. My father made it abundantly clear that he would allow me to do this for one school semester only, as training for my ministerial position. That was good enough for me. I would not only be able to be in a band and entertain for a living for a few months, I would be away from the hell he had made my life for a couple of short months, and with his blessing.

I toured with Young American Showcase for the semester in a band called Freedom Jam, learning more in those days about how to feel at ease in front of a crowd and how to front a show, than I had in my whole life.

It was truly some of the most exhausting work I'd ever done but I was having so much fun entertaining I didn't care about the long hours and endless driving, setting up and performing. We were performing three to five shows a day and I was learning how to sing rock music in front of large crowds and feel comfortable doing it. I had even incorporated ventriloquism, and the school kids and their teachers loved it.

This was what I had dreamed of since I was ten, when my teacher had spied me writing my name over and over hundreds of times in my notebook. He had asked me what I was doing and I matter-of-factly replied that I would be famous one day and I needed to practice my autograph.

Well, here I was doing shows for schools, and afterwards the kids would crowd around and want autographs. I was in heaven!

The president of Showcase, Lowell Lidell, gave me a great gift that year, unbeknownst to him. He was also a ventriloquist and saw me perform and gave me this advice: 'Don't allow the puppet to do too much talking because no matter how good you get you can't make it so your lips never move.' I felt the rebel in me stir. Oh really? I thought. OK then, I'll just work my butt off and make sure I get to the point where my lips never move. And that is exactly why my lips don't move. Don't try to tell me that I can't do something. I had spent a lifetime proving my dad wrong and I wasn't about to accept more terrible advice. Not if I have anything to say about it! Thanks, Lowell, for the advice. It has really helped me out!

We were paid very little money and got a miniscule amount of cash for food, but this was not about the riches—but about the experience. We worked hard and played harder. We used the opportunity to see as much of the country as we could on our days off. We went to the Grand Canyon, saw much of the Rocky Mountains, and toured Alberta, Canada, meeting many interesting folk along the road.

When my stint with Freedom Jam inevitably ended and I had to go back home to the drudgery of real work, I was miserable. The people at Young American Showcase had seen my potential as an entertainer and a singer, so they called and tried to persuade me to come back for another year, but no amount of begging and pleading and trying to convince my dad to let me, would cause him to give me his blessing on it, so I had to turn them down, much to my regret and misery.

I began to work on my dad's feelings about me starting my own band. I told him that I could make more money performing than we did cleaning, and that it would be a lot more fun. To my astonishment he agreed and I called up three of the guys I had met in Young American Showcase and they moved to Texas and we started a band, calling it TEXAS the band, and began learning country songs.

We had the attitude we adopted in Showcase, that as long as we were entertaining we could get away with anything, so we went to our first audition at a little bar in East Texas.

I wanted to make an impression so I carried Walter T. Airdale, my ventriloquist puppet, with me to the audition.

I'll never forget the shocked look on the owner of the bar's face as he opened the door and saw us standing there waiting to be let in to do the audition. Here we were, a bunch of long-haired guys (I had decided to grow out my hair since my miserable time at all those Christian schools that had forced me to wear a military cut), one of whom was holding a cowboy ventriloquist dummy, and I said, 'Hi, we're TEXAS the band and we want to audition to play here.' Walter said, 'Show us the stage and we'll knock your socks off!'

The bar owner didn't look amused. He showed us where to play and promptly sat down and started to talk to someone, facing away from us. We hadn't expected this. We were all about entertaining, and the band's musical abilities were, at best, terrible. The guys had really rushed the learning of the songs and slopped them out. In essence, we were terrible but we had counted on the club owner seeing how entertaining we were—but as he kept his back to us, he never saw that aspect. We didn't get the job. He told us to practice and come back in a few years.

One of the men who went to our church had a ranch (surprise!) and offered to let us use a shed there if we would work out on his ranch for a few days, and we agreed. We would spent a few hours a week helping him (oh, the horror!) and the rest of our time practicing in his shed. We actually learned to play songs reasonably well and set out to conquer the club circuit in Texas.

We went to a little biker bar named Pardners in Fairfield, Texas, and auditioned and got the job. We were ecstatic!

At Pardners we quickly became very popular due to our entertainment prowess, even though we only knew about twelve songs. We did fifteen-minute versions of songs like 'Sweet Home Alabama' and the drunk patrons thought it was great.

Since we had four hours of music to play every night for $500 a week, we had to play extended versions of every song until we finally learned enough music to fill up an entire night. We were spending every waking moment learning new country songs and rehearsing them, so eventually we could play all night and not repeat any songs at all. The owner of the bar asked us to be the house band for Pardners and Mad Hatters, a club in Palestine, Texas. We split the four-day week up, two nights in Palestine and two nights in Fairfield and quickly became a very popular draw to both bars, packing in patrons every night we played. The guys were not terribly good musicians, but we were extremely entertaining and had started to add some of our favorite rock songs to the show, not to mention the appearance of Walter T. Airdale, country singer extraordinaire, in every set.

In those days country bands made a lot more money in Texas than rock music so we didn't mind the compromise. Within a few months we were the hot ticket all over Texas.

Imagine this: you go out to see a country band, but not only do they play country music, they also infuse the show with great rock, comedy, and then the lead singer pulls out a ventriloquist puppet and the puppet flirts with the ladies and does a country song. It didn't take long before there were literally lines around the block. As if all this wasn't enough, the lead singer of this super-band would impersonate every single artist he did almost perfectly, whether the song was classic or modern country or modern rock.

Before long, the owner of the little club who had rejected us hired us and paid us more than he had ever paid a band before to play at his club, and we packed the place out night after night. He told us he was amazed at how quickly we had improved and was glad to have us. I was so proud at that moment, and I certainly wasn't bitter toward him.

I have never been one to have a chip on my shoulder for things like that. The fact was that we *didn't* deserve to play there when we had first auditioned. It was through our dedication and hard work that we had improved enough to be able to play there, and I knew it.

All of us in the band except for Jep (we hired him to play rhythm guitar for us to fill up the sound), had toured with Young American Showcase and had learned the art of entertaining—and my philosophy was that we should incorporate any and all talents we had into the band, regardless of how silly it may look, as long as it was entertaining. We were very energetic and funny, but as strict musicians, the band lacked greatly. For the sake of embarrassment I won't mention names of the band players except for Jep and myself. (I've asked Jep if he minds and he said, 'Go right ahead.')

We were a spectacularly entertaining group. Our drummer (although lacking in his ability to keep a steady beat) was a juggler and was able to actually juggle balls and other objects and balance a drum stick (which he later replaced with a rubber chicken—yes, I said a rubber chicken!) on his nose, all the while continuing to play the drums. Sure the beat was not perfect, but who cares? He was juggling and balancing stuff on his nose during the middle of the song.

Our bass player, although, in my opinion, very poor at the bass, was good-looking with flowing blond hair and very funny at times; he was one of the most entertaining people I had ever met. The ladies absolutely loved him, and he was a great strength to the persona of the band.

The guitar player was the real pretty-boy of the group, and while he was never the best guitar player around, he had a great feel for the instrument and learned to copy the riffs and leads of the great guitar players almost perfectly as the band progressed—he also had a decent singing voice, especially with background vocals.

I had no idea I was doing impressions during my years with TEXAS the band. I just thought if you learned a song you were supposed to do it like the original artist. It came so naturally I assumed everyone could do it. I was almost thirty years old and I went to a club to see another band with my guitar player. I was always annoyed that the singers rarely did a very good job and I figured they were trying to put their own stamp on it. I said to my guitar player, 'This guy is terrible. Why don't they just do it like the original artist?' and he looked at me like I was nuts. 'They can't!' he said, and I suddenly realized that I could do something quite unique.

We would go from a perfect Garth Brooks into a perfect Guns N' Roses song, then into George Strait, then into Def Leppard, after which Walter T. Airdale would come out and entertain. Droves of people would line up to see the show, but my father was quick to point out that the reason people loved us had very little to do with me. 'The real magic of your show is the band, it is the five of you together that makes you good,' he would constantly remind me, lest I begin to have too much confidence.

I bought it hook, line, and sinker. We continued to work and get better pay and better gigs, deciding to become a fully fledged show band instead of a bar act.

One day I said to my dad, 'I think it would be cool if I had Walter yodel.'

He immediately replied, 'It's impossible to learn to yodel. You either can't or you can. And you wouldn't be able to do it without moving your lips anyway, so give up the idea.'

I promptly went out and bought a Roy Rogers album (for the history-impaired among my readers I must point out that in the olden days we had vinyl recordings we called records. They were about ten times larger than CDs and we had to actually flip them over to hear the second half of the music). I worked for several months to learn to yodel without moving my lips.

I took a long time, but I finally mastered the skill. I just put it in the act one day when my father was there. He never mentioned it, but I always get a great feeling of satisfaction from that day.

I gave my heart and soul to the band, doing everything I could to make us the best I could. We had several chances to make it big and be signed to a major label, but my father refused to give up control of the creative process to anyone else, so we lost every opportunity to my dad's stupidity and stubbornness. I was still determined to make him proud of me by going along with his choices even when I knew he was wrong.

But in spite of his bad advice and insistence that we do things his way (invariably the wrong way) we did have a shot to sign with Warner Bros. Music in the early nineties. They were so interested they actually sent out a 'groomer' to travel with us and teach us how to be a signed band. He instructed us to quit doing the impersonations and I had to sing everything in my own voice. The rock music had to go. Country only, he told us. Also, the ventriloquism was 'ridiculous' as he put it, and had to go as well.

We lasted about three months under this new format, but I was so miserable and all of our new fans came to our shows expecting to see the dynamic, funny band they had fallen in love with and instead saw a cookie-cutter country band and left terribly disappointed. I can't tell you how many times I heard our fans saying, 'I brought out friends to see you guys but where was all the fun? Also, we missed Walter T.

Airdale. What's happened to you guys?' I hated it and for the first time since playing music I was ready to chuck it all and go back to cleaning houses.

We had a band meeting and decided to tell the record company to go jump. We figured that the entertainment and comedy was just as important to us as the music and, happily, resumed the comedy and ventriloquism, much to my delight. Yeah, it was our shot and we let it pass, but I never regretted the decision.

The greatest day of my life was when I was twenty-two years old, in 1989 and TEXAS the band was playing a show at the Chrystal Chandelier in Dallas.

I walked in to do the show just like any other night, but this time there was a gorgeous woman sitting with her back to me. She was wearing a purple sweater and when she turned to look at me our eyes locked. She was simply stunning and it was as if I had been struck by lightning! I felt my insides vibrating as I looked at her.

I had been attracted to many ladies up to this point in the band. In spite of the fact that I was not the pretty-boy of the band, or even the second best-looking guy we had, I did have my share of girls who had their crushes on me. Hey, if some of these rock stars can be considered a great-looking guy, I had some great chances as the lead singer of my own band!

My father had made the rule that none of us was allowed to date until the band made it big, mainly as a way of controlling us. He didn't want anyone else giving us outside advice, especially some silly girls.

I had made it a habit to sneak out of the house for late-night rendezvous with my female admirers, and I don't think my father ever suspected once that I had done this. I had become so good at snowing him into thinking I was completely under his thumb and control.

But this was diffcrent. Something inside me was really moved by this lady. I went up to her and introduced myself. Her name was Melinda. The only trouble was that I knew her friend (who had brought her to the show that night) had a crush on me. I danced a couple of times with Melinda's friend, all the while eyeing this angelic creature sitting at the table alone. The next week Melinda came to see us by herself and we danced during every break that night. She came to the show the next week and we did the same.

It was love at first sight, but I didn't want to admit it.

Melinda and I became very good friends over the next few months. She would come to as many shows as she could and we would talk and dance. She started to help us with our merchandise booth and became a good friend to all of the guys in the band.

One day we were playing at a club in Dallas and there was a guitar show in town, which the other guys in the band wanted to go to. I was left alone in the hotel room so I called Melinda and she came and picked me up. We watched a movie, *Bill and Ted's Excellent Adventure*, then went out to Grandy's and ordered chicken fried steak (I ate half of hers) and ended up at a park, sitting on a swing set and talking. I leaned over and kissed her. My emotions exploded as they never had before. I was consumed with feeling for her, and we ended up making out at the park until I had to get back to the room. We snuck out together a second time a few days later and went to see Disney's *The Little Mermaid*. To this day, *Bill and Ted's Excellent Adventure* and *The Little Mermaid* are two of my favorite movies. Any guesses why?

I explained to her that we had decided not to date anyone until the band hit it big, and she understood. I couldn't tell her then that it was really because I was afraid of my father's disapproval, but I eventually confided this to her.

I was sneaking out as often as I could to meet with her, and one night in a flash of realization I understood the truth. I was really and truly, unequivocally in love with her. I was absolutely terrified. I had no idea what I was going to do. It was one thing to meet late at night and go out for a burger or drive to the lake and sit hand in hand and talk for hours at a time, but I was really in love and I didn't want those nights to end. I wanted her to be with me all the time and I was scared to death.

I stopped calling her, since I didn't know how I would have enough courage to defy my parents and marry her. Melinda's heart was broken. She thought I was just another cad who had used her and dumped her, but I was suffering as much or more than she was, unbeknownst to her.

The days turned into weeks, and still I couldn't stand the thought of living without her, but I couldn't muster up the courage to call her and talk. She would come to some of our shows and I would try to be cordial, but I hid as well as I could the burning desire to take her in my arms.

After several weeks of misery and aching inside to tell her how I felt, I simply couldn't bear to be without her any longer. Convinced that she hated me and probably would never speak to me again, I took the plunge, finally couldn't take it anymore and I called her.

'Melinda, I'm in love with you and I don't know what to do about it,' I blurted out before she had a chance to say anything but 'Hello?'

She burst into tears and said, 'I thought you hated me. Why haven't you called?'

'I was scared,' I told her. 'I didn't know what to do about it. I have to defy my parents and I've never done that before, but I'm going to. I can't live without you.'

I told her I loved her about a hundred times that day,

and we both cried and professed our undying love for one another. Eighteen years later I still love her as much as I did the day I said those things. I guess it was for real.

I finally went to my parents and told them about Melinda. They threw a fit and screamed and yelled, threatening me with everything they could think of but I said it didn't matter; I wanted to be with her and that was that. I could quit the band and move out if they liked, but they didn't like the idea of having to go back to cleaning for a living, so they finally agreed and Melinda joined our family.

As the band continued to progress, Melinda became my heart and soul. She would come to the shows and my heart would just burst with love every time I saw her.

We went to the Texas State Fair together shortly after all of this, and went up into the Texas Star, a huge ferris wheel, and as we got to the top we kissed. We still do that every year at the fair if I find myself not touring and able to go.

She became my light in the middle of much darkness because, although I was fronting a fabulous band and touring the country, my father still had complete control of my life. But now I had someone who loved me and who was mine, and it made my heart soar.

One day, as we lay together on the floor watching a movie with the other band members surrounding us, she took a pair of diamond earrings out of her ears and then removed my little cheap earrings (hey, give me a break, it was the early '90s and I was a long-hair in a country-rock band—it was supposedly cool!) and put her own earrings into my ears. It was one of nicest moments of my entire life. I felt that there and then we formed a real bond.

A few months later we were walking hand in hand at a Sam's Club outlet and I offhandedly said, 'We are going to get married, aren't we?'

'Of course!' came her reply, and that is the romantic tale of how I proposed.

I didn't feel that it was quite as romantic as it could have been, so, being poor and unable to get her a nice ring on my own, I took the precious earrings she had given me to a jeweler and asked them to put the diamonds into a ring for her, and when we were at the entrance to Scarborough Fair (a renaissance fair in Waxahachie, Texas) I got on one knee and held up the cheap ring to her and asked her to be my wife.

I'm not sure which she is most embarrassed about, the fact that I first proposed in a Sam's Club or that I did it again officially in front of (geek that I am) a renaissance festival. I know she is mortified that these details are now public information, but I know you all would like to know the story. Sorry, honey, you married a geek.

Anyway, a few months later we were in Denver doing a show (Melinda had started traveling with us to run our merchandise booth and sound) and I said to her, 'Hey, want to get married today?'

'Sure!' she replied, and we went, applied for the license, and were married by a Justice of the Peace at the court house in Denver, Colorado. As I had no money to buy her a ring, we just used her engagement ring.

A couple of weeks later we were in Las Vegas and I bought her a wedding ring at a pawn shop for $10. She was quite happy and content with it for years, but I was secretly ashamed of the fact that I had not been able to get her a nice ring.

After I won a million dollars on *America's Got Talent*, we were in a mall one day and I took her to a jewelry store to buy her a watch and walked out with a spectacular ring, in spite of her protests. I told her it was more for me than her and confessed my shame, much to her surprise. She said she had always been proud of her ring and had never even once thought twice about it. I'm so lucky.

After we married we had no money to move into our own house so we had to live with my parents, much to our horror. Everything the band made went into the community bank so we had nothing of our own. I thought maybe being a married man perhaps my father would treat me more as an adult, but it didn't happen. My father would still scream and yell at me for hours at a time, regularly bursting into our room in the middle of the night telling me what a useless waste of space I was, but now I had someone who would, in the darkness that followed, tell me that the things he said weren't true.

Melinda also began to say things like, 'Terry, you do realize that the reason people like this band so much is because of what you do for it, don't you?'

Of course, that was ridiculous. The magic was the whole band. There were five of us and it was the combination of the five that attracted people. I had very little to do with it, I thought, but Melinda continued to try to boost my self-confidence, no easy feat in light of how battered my self-image was from the constant emotional berating I was taking from my dad.

We had hired an agency to book us, and Brian (the president of the agency) would parrot my father constantly. 'The magic is the whole group. No-one is more important than the rest. All five of you together are why you are successful.' Again, I bought it. I felt that alone, I would be a complete failure, and without all of us, I was nothing.

We pooled all our money together to pay the bills and no-one really had anything that belonged to them during those years. Melinda and I moved out of my parents' house and into a house with my brother (Jep played rhythm guitar for us) and his wife, Pam. It wasn't horrible but there was no way to have a sense that we were making our own lives or doing anything for our futures. Debi married the guitar player and they lived with my mom and dad and the bass player and drummer.

Darrell Johnson (remember him? The guy I stayed with when I was seventeen and got kicked out of my house) had become a close friend of the band and I asked him to utilize his prowess as a producer and director to help us put together a killer show, and we spent the entire summer writing, rehearsing and building something absolutely amazing.

We toured for a couple of years, playing the fair circuits and packing out club after club with our blend of comedy and impersonations. I was doing the Michael Jackson impressions I had done in college (without the silly change in the lyrics) to great success, as well as anything else we could think of that was entertaining.

One night we were performing at a club we had been house band at for the past six months and bored with the same old routine, we started to do crazy things on stage just to shake things up.

I finished my Michael Jackson impression as usual, but this time I didn't change out of the coat I wore. I began to talk in my squeaky, high Michael Jackson voice about how much I loved country music and how the greatest influence I had ever had was a country legend named Walter T. Airdale, and I proceeded to get him. Walter began to make fun of Michael Jackson, after which Michael and Walter sang a country song together, with me singing it in Michael Jackson's voice and Walter doing it like Hank Williams, much to the delight of the crowd and the band—and a new routine was born. I still do that routine to this day.

We were very successful but the commune-type existence didn't give any of us a chance to feel as though we were doing anything to build a future for ourselves.

Everything we did was for the common good of the entire group (at least, we kept telling ourselves that) until we made the big time. We had dreams of making it, and finally getting houses of our own, but it didn't seem to be happening, and we continued to struggle with our daily needs and expenses.

Why Melinda stayed with me during those times I'll never know. She stood beside me no matter how horrible the situation, constantly reminding me of my value and my talent, and I'll always appreciate her for it. I have many people tell me to thank her for never letting me give up, and I do pass on their messages to her, but most will never understand just how much she has meant to me, both professionally and personally.

Our niece Alyssa traveled with us and was home-schooled on the bus and it was such a joy to have her around. She brought such a fresh perspective to our hectic lives. Once when she was about four years old we were in a rush to get to a show and made a quick stop for dinner. As we were hurrying into the restaurant Alyssa saw some flowers growing in a little flower-bed outside the restaurant and she stopped and bent down to smell them. It was such a profound 'Stop and smell the roses' moment for me.

She became so special to us and we enjoyed having her with us, even though the life of a gypsy can't have been easy for her as she, like her father, uncle and aunt, never had the chance to set down roots and just have friends and schooling like a normal kid. I know it was selfish to need her, but I honestly don't know if I could have made it through all those years without her child's innocence and perspective of the world. We all adored her and doted on her constantly.

The first to finally get tired of the commune-type existence we lived was the drummer. He found himself a girlfriend and quit the band immediately, which didn't affect us at all. We were still just as much a draw as we ever were.

'It's the four of you that makes the magic. Without the group you wouldn't be anything!' became the new line from my father and Brian.

~

My mother had finally had enough of my dad's controlling and left as well, filing for divorce.

In her several attempts to damage my father she did many things that hurt us terribly—trying to take away my dad's sole financial support—and in the process damaged her relationship with all three of her children, irreparably with my wife.

I have since restored contact with my mom, understanding that sometimes we can be driven to extremes by our circumstances, and as happens in too many divorces, the offspring become caught in the middle. My mother had decided that the best way to destroy my father's only source of income was to ruin the band. As a result she leveled attacks at us and our reputations, thinking that if we lost all of our business my father would suffer. I was terribly hurt by these attacks and as a result said hurtful things back to her in retaliation. I have forgiven her but some wounds are too deep to fix and I fear they may never heal fully. I think I understand that these wounds are simply more carnage of my father's narcissism and dementia, because he has left emotionally battered and bruised people behind him everywhere he has gone, and my relationship with my mother is just another of those casualties.

We hired Brian as our manager and he decided to make a final blow to my ego, in spite of the fact that I never felt I was all that instrumental to our success. He set up a meeting with the whole band.

I had developed a condition called Chronic Fatigue Syndrome. Our grueling schedule, which included several hours a day of set-up and tear-down of our gear as well as three-plus hours of entertaining had caused me to collapse several times. I was laid up for days, and sometimes weeks, sometimes even needing help to go to the rest room because I didn't have the energy to walk by myself.

My doctor told me that I had to change my schedule or I might end up losing my career—or even my life. I was the kind of entertainer who put all the strength and energy I had into every second I was on stage, then continue to push the limits day after day, night after night, and I simply couldn't physically keep up the pace, so my body would shut itself down in order to force me to rest.

My doctor told me I had to make a choice: if I wanted to perform I had to stop the set-up and tear-down of the gear. Otherwise I could just be a roadie, but I couldn't do both. I told the band that I had to rest before and after shows and that was that. For a long time I felt guilty about it, like I wasn't doing my part for the band, but it was the only choice I had; it was just the way things were.

Brian didn't see it that way. He didn't believe that I had any physical problems at all and was just not pulling my weight with the band. After all, how could I possibly do our shows with such gusto and energy if I truly had physical limitations?

We arrived at the meeting they set up and he began to tell me I wasn't doing enough for the band and that I needed to shape up and contribute more. I pretty much *was* the show except for the times I needed to take a short break and let one of the other guys sing a song. We were playing two and three hours a night and I couldn't handle the strain vocally.

The bass player stood up and began to shout at me that I took and took from the band and never gave anything back. Everyone ganged up on me to vent their frustrations. Until that moment I never knew what it felt to have my heart absolutely torn from my chest. I was devastated. I had given my heart and soul to this band and knew in my very core that I had nothing more to give it. I began to weep. All of the years of criticism had finally taken its toll. I felt that no matter what I did I could never do enough. No matter how hard I worked and how good I got, I would never receive any credit for any of it.

I left the room and found Melinda and Debi in complete confusion. Why was I sobbing so desperately? Through my wracking sobs I told them what had transpired and they were both furious. Debi asked Jep why he had not at least defended me. Later I talked with him about it and he feels terrible about the whole thing, but had really got caught up in the situation. I forgive him of course (he's a really good guy), but I know that Melinda and Debi never forgot what my bass player and Brian did to me that day.

Brian was furious at my reaction and his wife told Debi that she needed to support her husband (who had sat in stony silence during the meeting) and not her brother, to which she replied that if he would not be so stupid she would. I like Debi!

As difficult as this was to have happen, it led to the second greatest event in my life.

My father had decided that he had had enough, and wanted to commit suicide. He announced it to me, Debi and Jep and gave us a date that he would take his life.

I had no idea how to take this news, but I did know that I didn't want him to end it all until I had his approval, and until I could catch that elusive white rabbit I had chased my whole life. I determined that I would do anything I could to make sure he told me he was proud of me before he ended it all.

I dedicated myself to become anything he wanted me to become, to surrender my own identity so that I could finally win his approval.

For more than a month I gave him anything he wanted. At one point he told me Monty Python wasn't funny, so I threw all of my Monty Python CDs in the trash, agreeing with him that they weren't funny. I became intolerable to the rest of my family, but I didn't care. I had to have my father's approval before he died, and I didn't care what the consequences were. I was more miserable than I had ever been, but I didn't care. *Just a few more days*, I would think. *I can do this. My dad will finally be proud of me! Just keep going, almost there!*

The day finally arrived when my father was to take his own life, and he got his three children before him, telling Debi and Jep what disappointments they had always been to him.

He said that the only one of his children he was proud of was Terry. 'This last month Terry has proven how much he loves me,' he said. 'He is the only one I am proud of.'

I'm sure these words hurt Jep and Debi, but I didn't think about that; I only cared that the hell I had been through, the complete loss of my own will and self, would soon be over, and I had accomplished exactly what I had set out to.

I had finally done it! I had won his approval, and soon he would be gone and I could think for myself again and know that he had died saying he was proud of me.

Debi tells me now that during that month I was intolerable, that for the only time in her entire life she really couldn't stand me. I only cared what my dad thought, and since my father cares about nothing but himself, I became a person who thought only of him and no-one else. He has never cared about anyone or anything beyond his own desires and wants. I was finally the person he wanted me to be, a person who worshipped him and agreed that every thought he had was brilliant, raving on and on about how wise he was and what a great man he was.

The only trouble is that my father is not a nice person. He is a selfish, terrible man, and in order to become his disciple I had to treat others with the same contempt *he* had for them, Debi and Jep included.

I have no idea why or how Melinda stayed with me through that month. I can only guess that she knew how important it was for me to win my father's approval, and she patiently waited for me to return to my former self, the one she had fallen in love with.

To act like I did was opposite to my own personality. I like people, my father hates people. I think people are basically good, he thinks everyone is evil. If a room is too cold and someone complains about it, I would rather be too warm than for someone else to be uncomfortable. My father cares nothing at all about anyone else in the room but what *he* wants.

In order to gain his approval I had to do anything and everything he wanted, at the expense of everyone else.

The night of his impending suicide was not one of heaviness and sadness for me; it was one of great relief that my personal hell was almost over. I could resume my life again and be a nice guy once more.

My father took a bunch of pills and ended up getting sick, throwing up all night. He survived.

I was heartsick. I knew I couldn't live under his rule anymore. I felt like I had lost part of my soul during that horrible month, but my father was completely oblivious to the fact that it had all been a play to get his approval. He honestly thought I had seen the error of my ways and had discovered what a great man he was, and that was why I had kissed his butt all those weeks. After a couple of days he recovered and couldn't understand why I no longer wanted to do everything he said. He told me that I had to work on my attitude and that if I wanted to go to heaven, I had to continue to surrender my identity to his whims.

I couldn't do it. Reluctantly, I saw the rabbit I thought I had secured forever, wriggle out of my hands once again and scurry down the rabbit hole, mocking me as he went.

I left the house my dad was in and went to talk to Melinda and Debi.

'I guess I'm going to hell because I can't do this anymore, I simply cannot be the person my father wants from me.'

Melinda came up to me and wrapped me in her arms as Debi said, 'You aren't going to hell, Terry. God won't abandon you.'

'Well, I know this, if God had chosen an ass like our dad to be His representative, I think I'd rather spend and eternity in hell away from Him because He must not be a very nice God.'

Melinda laughed for the first time in more than a month.

Both of them told me it was nice to have me back.

My dad walked into the room and demanded that I apologize. I said to him, 'I can't do it anymore. I like myself. Melinda loves me. Debi loves me. I'm just going to be myself from now on. I'm through with you and everything you stand for!'

My father was stunned. I had never stood up to him like that. I told him that I was no longer going to allow him to run my life or my band and that it was over.

He began to scream and shout but to no avail. Then he pulled the God card out. 'You do realize that by defying me God will send you to hell?'

And I dropped the bomb on him. 'I know,' I replied. 'I choose hell over a life under you any longer. If heaven means that I have to spend eternity with you telling me what I can and can't do, then hell will be a welcome relief!'

I might have actually left God then and there and I was severely tempted to just hang it all up and become an atheist, but in spite of the fact that I never felt God calling me to be a minister, I really did have a heart for Him. I loved Him and didn't want to lose Him from my life.

In spite of the words I had said I was absolutely devastated that I might lose God's blessing in my life, so I went to the quiet of my room and prayed.

'God,' I said softly, *'I really do love you and I don't want to lose you but I have reached a breaking point in my life. I can no longer serve my father. He has told me since I was a child that if I didn't have his blessing I couldn't have you either. I need to know.'* I picked up a quarter. *'I believe you can control even the flip of a coin. I am going to flip this quarter. If it comes up heads, I know that my father is wrong and that you love me and I will love you back until my dying day, but know this: I will never again let another human being try to tell me your will for me. If you want me to know something you have to tell me yourself. I will know that I can have a relationship with you and have your blessing even without my dad's blessing. If the quarter comes up tails then I know you have abandoned me and my father is right. I will turn away and never bother you again, knowing that I have chosen against you, but I cannot live under my dad's rule anymore.'*

I was heartbroken that I might really lose God, but it was a chance I had to take. I flipped the coin and it came up heads. A flood of happiness washed over me and I knew it was done. I could have God *and* defy my father orders and wishes.

Until that moment, the happiest single experience of my life had been the day I looked at Melinda and said 'I do', but this was comparable to even that exhilaration. I felt truly free. In the split-second of that coin spinning and flashing and landing on my hand with the head gleaming up at me, I had been set free of decades of oppression and fear. It may seem silly and simple to have put such a large stock in such a tiny moment, but until you have been under that type of oppression you can't understand what it can mean.

I promptly went out and told my dad what I had done, and of course he protested. 'You were sinning just by even asking that question. You knew the answer beforehand. You can't have God without me.' I smiled and said, 'Well He seems to think I can.' I walked out. I was free.

Most people at this point would simply never have anything more to do with someone like my dad, but it is my nature to be forgiving and to not write anyone off. For a long time my contact with my father was minimal, but I knew that if I cut off from him entirely I may regret it one day so I made a decision to extend the olive branch and chose to speak to him.

A few years later I told my dad that I wanted to be friends with him, but that it would be on my terms, not his. He still had the annoying habit of screaming at me any time I disagreed with him on anything. His opinions were the only ones that mattered to him and anyone who felt differently was an idiot. I told him that as an adult we could be friends and have a relationship, but that he had to start accepting I was a smart individual and that my opinions were valid. We could discuss things, but I would not tolerate his outbursts anymore. He walked away and I never saw him again.

Alice's white rabbit had always eluded me, and now I knew he would never be mine, but he had become much fainter over the past few years and I had learned to ignore him. Maybe I didn't need to catch him.

I thought it was all over, but last year after I won *America's Got Talent* (I still have not heard from him in spite of my success and don't expect to and hope I don't) I was driving along in my home town Dallas when a song came on the radio by Vertical Horizon called 'I'm Still Here'.

I found the pieces in my hand, the song played.
They were always there it just took some time for
*   me to understand*
You gave me words I just can't say
So if nothing else I'll just hold on while you drift
*   away*
'Cause everything you wanted me to hide
Is everything that makes me feel alive
The cities grow the rivers flow
Where you are I'll never know but I'm still here
If you were right and I was wrong

Why are you the one who's gone and I'm still here
Still here

I had never heard the song before and as I listened to the words the years of grief suddenly burst forth in a flood of weeping and tears. I pulled the car over and gripped the steering wheel and my entire body was convulsing as I sobbed and the song played.

I've seen the ashes in my heart
I smile the widest
When I cry inside and my insides blow apart
I tried to wear another face
Just to make you proud
Just to make you put me in my place
'Cause everything you wanted from me
Is everything that I could never be.

(Even as I write the words now my eyes are brimming with tears remembering the crushing emotion I felt the first time I heard it.)

The chorus played again, saying everything for me as I sat and wept ever harder.

The cities grow the rivers flow
Where you are I'll never know but I'm still here
If you were right and I was wrong
Why are you the one who's gone and I'm still here
Still here
Maybe tonight it's gonna be all right I will get
    better
Maybe today it's gonna be okay I will remember

The cars around me continued to flash by in a blur, as I was oblivious to the rest of the world and allowed myself to truly let go in a way I had never thought possible. The power of the lyrics had consumed me as the song spoke to my soul and told me that I had made the right choices in my life and that I had done okay with myself. I *was* still here. I had continued in my own path and had not been destroyed by my own choices as my father had constantly predicted.

I sat crying my eyes out as the song continued to speak the words I had not been able to formulate in my own head for so many years.

> *I held the pieces of my soul*
> *I was shattered*
> *And I wanted you to come and make me whole*
> *Then I saw you yesterday*
> *But you didn't notice*
> *You just walked away*
> *'Cause everything you wanted me to hide*
> *Is everything that makes me feel alive*

The chorus played one last time as my body continued to sob and convulse under the crushing weight of my emotion.

> *The cities grow the rivers flow*
> *Where you are I'll never know but I'm still here*
> *If you were right and I was wrong*
> *Why are you the one who's gone and I'm still here*

And then the final tag to the song spoke even more what I knew to be true and I wept ever harder at the certainty and the finality of it all.

The lights go out
The bridge is burned
Once you go you can't return
But I'm still here
Remember how you used to say I'd be the one to run
    away but I'm still here
I'm still here
I'm still here

Yes, I'm still here. All of my father's insults, lies and control melted away as the song finished. I turned off the radio and sat listening to the rush of the traffic. I sat for about ten minutes and composed myself. The white rabbit that I had chased for so long and dreamed of one day catching had grown ever fainter, and in my mind's eye he finally vanished. I think we were both relieved; he to be free of the pursuit, and I of the dream.

⌒

Oops! Sorry, there's the ADD again. See how I just jumped ahead and told a story out of chronological order? Welcome to the ADD-addled mind. Weird, isn't it? Melinda has tried to understand it all our lives together, but she just can't get it.

I have jumped a little ahead of myself but I sort of got carried away by the emotion and happiness of this great moment in my life. I think it's time I got back into the timeline of the story. I hope I didn't ruin the ending.

Let's see, where was I? Oh, yes!

After a few more months Jep quit the band so he could start his own life. He and Pam and Alyssa moved away and he pursued his own dreams. He went back to school and became a control systems engineering technician. He has made quite a success of himself and I am so proud of him.

Once again, though, it had no effect on the band's success. Same amount of bookings. Same amount of money, but only three members instead of four or five. The new mantra was, 'It's the three of you that make the magic. Without you three you'd be nothing.'

I still didn't get it. You'd think by now I'd have a clue that Melinda was right when she told me that the reason we were so successful was because of my contribution, but I couldn't accept it. I was nothing more than a simple cog in the wheel, without the whole of which I was nothing.

We struggled along for a few more years, but the call of a solo career was getting more and more urgent. I felt that I wasn't living up to my true dream of being a professional ventriloquist, but I was too scared of letting go of the notion that I needed the others to be a success.

Finally it had all come to a head. The band members finally announced that they were sick of doing the comedy and ventriloquism and wanted to play bars and just do music. We were earning the top amount of money you could make playing fairs and festivals around the country, but they were tired of the show band aspect and wanted to just be musicians.

I was frightened, but Melinda kept assuring me that I would be just as successful by myself without all of the dead weight, and I could keep all the money for myself. That was certainly attractive, but what if no-one wanted me? What if Brian and my dad had been right? What if the only reason people liked us was because of the 'magic' of the group? I had so many doubts and absolutely no confidence.

When the band would showcase for fairs, we would play about twenty minutes for a state fair convention to demonstrate what we did. Afterwards we'd always have lines of people waiting to book us.

The band members went their separate ways, and in typical musician fashion, the guitar player announced to Debi that he wanted to pursue his music with the bass player and he abandoned her. I mean, he literally abandoned her. He never sent her a cent for support. He even made her pay for the divorce, in spite of the fact that she is disabled and lives on a fixed income. A real winner, him.

How I ever thought I needed him to be successful I'll never know, but I had been so brainwashed by those around me, especially my father, my confidence was completely shot. I took the next few weeks to write a showcase. I have mentioned in an early chapter that my father had told me I was a terrible writer when I was ten and that I dealt with it later on in life—and now I'll tell you exactly how I did deal with it.

The psychological poison my father had injected into me when he said those simple words had infected me to the core. I couldn't write no matter how hard I tried. I couldn't seem to allow myself to come up with ideas. I would think that it's just not my forte and I should just give it up. But one day Melinda (bless her) asked me if I thought hypnosis would help. I had studied hypnosis to help Debi with her pain, so I thought I'd give it a shot on myself.

I did a self-hypnosis session and pictured my father having built a giant brick wall inside my mind that had hardened, and which I couldn't get past. Behind that wall was all the creativity I would ever need to be a great writer and comedian. In my mind I took a sledge hammer and began to tear the wall down. I spent a lot of time making sure there was nothing left of that wall. When I finished I found that not only could I write, I could write well!

I was able to be more creative and productive and began to write very inventive and clever routines, each of which I am as proud of as I can be!

I finally had my own act and I set up a fair showcase as a solo act.

I went out on stage terrified because now it was all on my own shoulders. I would sink or swim on my own steam and there was no-one left to blame if things went sour.

I had completely started my life over and I was in my late thirties. I'd had to reinvent my entire act, and was doing new characters and material that I had written myself over the past few months.

I was about to find out whether Melinda had been right. Had it really been me that had drawn the crowds and the work, or had it been the 'magic' of our group.

I felt sick to my stomach as I took the stage.

I looked out at the crowd, feeling alone and naked. I had not done solo shows since I was very young and had absolutely zero confidence in my ability to command an audience without the surrounding support of my band mates. I had been told for so long that I was not important to our success that I really thought I would bomb out.

I took a deep breath as I looked out over the audience and launched into my routine.

I had no music in my act at the time; I was just doing comedy routines with puppets the way every other ventriloquist act you might have seen would do, but my routines were clever and innovative and my characters were fully fleshed and three dimensional. Years earlier I had seen fellow ventriloquist, Ronn Lucas, on the Disney Channel and he had raised the bar for me about how good I could get.

I had decided that even if I couldn't be better than him (he's about as good as you can be technically) I would at least strive to be as good as him. I worked hours and hours to make sure my puppets truly came alive and seemed like real entities. I decided that my routine would be a talk show and I would be the host, with my puppets as the guests.

I finished my routine and received thunderous applause and a standing ovation, and then went back to the room to find it packed out with booking agents.

Same amount of bookings, a little less money, but I had done it alone and I didn't have to split it up several ways. It was all my money to do with as I pleased!

Believe me, Melinda loved that for the first time in our married lives I was bringing home a real pay check and was able to contribute to our bills.

It *had* been my talent that had been the attraction! I was stunned beyond belief.

After I won *America's Got Talent* and the price for my solo show had far eclipsed the most the whole band had ever even dreamed of making, the band's old manager, Brian, booked me again for a corporate gig, amazed at how much I was charging for the one night as a solo act.

I did the show and the clients came up and raved about how it was the best show they had ever had at their corporate event, and they had no idea how they would ever top it the following year.

Brian said to me afterwards that I should consider a reunion tour with the band. 'I could really book you guys if you'd get back together. You guys really had a magic.'

I just smiled. He still doesn't get it, but at least *I* do now.

It's all right, though. He can't afford me anymore.

Chapter 7

Flying Solo

Gosh it sure sounds like I'm a weepy kind of guy, doesn't it? Reading over all this it sure sounds like I cry at the drop of a hat, but the truth is that I find it very difficult to cry. I think the only times I have ever wept hard are during the writing of this book; even when I won America's Got Talent I almost cried but didn't, although I do tear up when I watch romantic comedies, my favorite type of movie. I know, I know, I'm a big wuss (a word from the '80s generation meaning girly-man), but I can't help it. I love romantic comedies. Like any other guy I enjoy the big–budget action flicks, and I do love goofy Adam Sandler-type comedies, but I prefer romantic comedies to all of them. And I tear up at every one of them.

All right, enough about what a wimp I am, let's get back to our story.

I sent a copy of the last chapter of this book to my brother Jep and asked him to comment on it. He told me he had no idea of how picked-on I felt and that he had never had any ill feelings toward me and I believe him. He was by far the hardest worker in the band as it was his job to fix the bus any time it broke down. One time he had to tear the bus apart and find an electrical short, then he restored it to like new. He was a very dedicated guy and I appreciate him more than he knows.

As I look back on the years with the band I see how dedicated Jep was to our success, and though there were difficult times I feel grateful to him for his perseverance and work ethic. I have never resented him for anything that happened during those years.

He told me he was amazed at how different my perspective was from his own, and that his memory of all these events was radically different from my own, but isn't that how it always is? My memories are different from everyone else's who were there because my perspective is my own. I can only remember my own emotions and feelings of an experience in my own life, and that is what I am expressing to you in this book. Sometimes it's hard for us to remember that we are in a sense in our own world and that no one else experiences exactly what we experience. Even Debi commented on this when she read the part I wrote about her getting her hand held over a flame by my father. She said she had never thought about how it must have felt to be me, helpless to do anything to aid her in her pain. As someone writes about their own experiences I think it's easy for others to say, 'That's not how it happened!' But, of course, it may be how it happened to the one telling it. What an interesting thought…

~

So once again I have been distracted and my timelines are flopping around like a Mexican jumping bean, and once again I must return to the tale of my life.

I was now embarking on a solo career which I had proven I could do, but was woefully unprepared for. In spite of the fact that I had impressed the buyers and I had secured a lot of work for the following summer, I had the one small detail of actually writing and memorizing a show that people would enjoy.

Excitedly I began to work on it, trying to cull as much from my years with the band as I could, deciding to keep the Michael Jackson bit in, taking this routine and that, writing new ones where I needed. I had also written an entire album of original music, and I wrote comedy routines that incorporated the songs into them so I could sing my own stuff and hopefully sell a few CDs as well.

I soon had about an hour's worth of material, enough to do two thirty-minute shows. Since the fairs I played had hired me to do three thirty-minute shows, I figured I could repeat the first one during my third time slot, and it worked out perfectly. Most entertainers at the fairs only have one routine that they repeat several times a day, so it was unusual that I actually had two different shows.

I was a big hit and almost every fair I played signed me up to play the following year as well. Not one to rest on my laurels, I continued to write more material, and before my first year of solo entertaining was over I had three separate half-hour shows put together.

One night shortly after I started my solo career, I was driving on my way to Florida to play at a fair and I had an extremely odd experience. Not one to have ever had a truly supernatural event, I was quite taken aback by what happened.

I was staying at a hotel in Mississippi and I had just drifted off to sleep when I suddenly found myself floating above my house in Mesquite, Texas. I wasn't alone but I have no idea who or what was next to me, but they could communicate with me.

The being asked me if I knew what I was looking at.

'I do,' I replied. 'That's my house down there but it is empty and there is no roof on it.'

I could see the entire layout of the house from my perspective above it.

'Good. What else do you see?'

'Well, I see a huge empty barrel in the middle of the living room. There is a giant faucet over it and it is dripping water into the barrel,' I continued.

'Excellent. Do you understand what it means?' the being asked.

I tried to figure it out, but couldn't, and I told the being so.

'The house and the water drum represent your life, and the faucet is the blessing you are receiving. Notice how the faucet is blocked and unable to run freely. If it were turned on at full force and the blockage were to be destroyed here is what would happen.'

Immediately the faucet began to gush water and the barrel filled up instantaneously, overflowing onto the carpet and filling the whole house with water. Then it began spilling out of the house and into the streets until the entire neighborhood was flooding.

'The blockage represents the bitterness you are holding on to toward those who have wronged you. If you will let go of that hatred and bitterness the blockage will be removed and you will be blessed beyond your wildest dreams, and you will be a blessing to everyone around you as well,' the being said matter of factly.

I looked at the flooding house for what seemed like a few seconds and then I was waking up in my bed at the little motel. My heart was racing from the fresh dream and I immediately called Melinda, even though the hour was very late.

She answered, and I stammered on about the amazing crazy dream I had just had and told her that I wasn't sure if it wasn't more of a vision than a dream. It had seemed so real.

I told Melinda I was going to do what the being had instructed me to do and that I was going to forgive everyone who had wronged me, and no longer harbor bitterness in my heart at all.

I was able to accomplish this over the next few months, and I came to understand that forgiving someone who has wronged you many times in the past doesn't necessarily mean I had to invite them back into my life to continue their wrongdoing, just that I would truly forgive them and not hold hatred toward them.

Earlier I said that I have not heard from my father and hoped I didn't. I was not speaking in bitterness. I have truly forgiven him, but he has literally left a pathway of bruised and broken people in his wake everywhere he has gone for as long as I have been alive, and I simply will not ever give him the chance to do it again to me. But I have nothing against him and I do not wish ill on him at all. He will just never be a part of my life again in any fashion because of his need to hurt people.

Melinda didn't know what to think of it all, but she said that whatever I decided was fine with her and I went back to sleep.

I continued to tour and perform all over the country and send the money back to Melinda. I was having a great time.

Several years earlier (when I was still with the band) I had gotten into the doldrums of work and had grown very weary of doing shows day after day and was very bored with my job. I think this happens to most other people and is not that unusual. I was watching TV one night and a movie came on called *The Jolson Story*, based on the life story of Al Jolson.

It was a life-changing moment for me as I saw his passion for performing and I realized that I had shared that passion my entire life. It was as though I had woken up from a deep sleep and realized that I was doing what I had always dreamed of. Even though I wasn't famous, I still had the talent to get up in front of crowds and sing and entertain, and from the moment I saw that movie I have never taken for granted that I am getting to do what I have loved and ached to do my whole life.

I even started to enjoy entertaining small groups of people, and would always bring a puppet to every party I went to, encouraging Melinda to let everyone know I was a ventriloquist. I still love to do that to this very day, although I don't have to have to get Melinda to tell anyone what I do anymore; they already know!

Anyway, in spite of the fact that I was playing very small stages at county fairs, I loved every minute of it. Being a solo act was great. No more arguments about where we were going to eat, no more pleading and begging and yelling to get the guys to rehearse; if I wanted to write and learn a new act, I just did it. It was so wonderful to know that the quality of my show was dependent on me alone.

I am one of the most laid-back people you will ever meet. While my father demanded perfection from everyone but himself I really didn't make a big deal out of much except my work. One thing I demand is that I give every bit of myself to the audience every time I set foot on stage, and I felt the same way about the band. Now I didn't have to worry about the other members of the band any more; I was in complete control, and it was heaven.

Unfortunately my agent had no contacts other than fairs, and once that season ended I had no way to make any money. I would spend the off-season picking up odd jobs, raking leaves, painting houses, anything I could do to bring in a little extra cash. I tried to drum up business by sending out flyers to booking agents, but had no luck at all.

I was trying my best to make enough to take some of the pressure off Melinda financially, but I couldn't seem to do it, so I was left to find as many odd jobs as I could, just to eke out a living. But I continued to work on my act and write as much new material as I could and perfect it before the next fair season.

No amount of begging and pleading with my agent could get her to find me work outside of the fair season. She was able to get me a couple of shows in Florida during the winter months, but couldn't get me steady work.

Melinda kept telling me that anyone with my talent shouldn't have to paint houses, and luckily the agents I found agreed with her! I started to fill my years playing fairs, corporate dates, theaters, and more.

One of my agents asked me what I thought of playing for schools since he had made a contact with QSP, a fund-raising program connected with *Reader's Digest*. They had secured me a showcase with the representatives.

I thought it would be great to be able to play for schools and did the showcase. I was a huge success and began playing for all different ages from kindergarten to high school, bringing messages about anti-bullying and drug and alcohol abuse.

I was now working more than I had ever dreamed, and loving every minute of it.

It was in the summer of 2005 that again my life and career changed.

I was doing a couple of impressions like Michael Jackson in my show but not many. In those days Michael Jackson had gone on trial and I tried to take the impression out of my show because I felt it was in bad taste. The fans at my shows were very upset at me for this and would tell me that they had brought friends to see it and begged me to put it back in the show. I obliged by asking every audience whether or not they wanted me to do my Michael Jackson impression. They always said yes.

I had seen many karaoke-type singers on the fair circuit, and it always seemed a little unprofessional to me to stand up in front of a crowd and sing to tracks, and I refused to do it. I was doing mainly comedy routines and the Michael Jackson bit with an original song thrown in to help sell CDs, but that was it.

I had done impressions with my puppets several years earlier in my band but it never seemed that amazing. I had Walter sing like Dwight Yoakum and Hank Williams, Sr. but no one ever made a big deal out of it so I took it out of the show.

So, in spite of the fact that I had been an impressionist for years and had even had one of my characters do impressions, it never seemed to be that important.

One day I thought about reviving the old routine of having a puppet do an impression. This time it was a different character than Walter. I decided to do it on the fly with no rehearsal, something I absolutely never did, but for some reason I was curious to find out if I had the ability to do it. I figured that if it didn't work I could ad-lib a few lines about how bad the puppet was and move on. I had developed a routine with an Elvis puppet in which he told me that he was the best Elvis impersonator in the world, but it turned out he didn't actually know any Elvis songs. The routine ended with him (his name is Maynard Thompkins) telling me, after I demanded that he name one Elvis song he could do, that he knew 'Friends in Low Places'.

It was a cute routine and one that I had done for years, but it always ended with me exasperated and taking Maynard off in a huff, but that night I decided to change the ending by challenging Maynard. Little did I realize that I was about to do something that would create another change in my life even though it still took a few more years for it to happen.

I had an iPod and had loaded several of my favorite karaoke versions of songs I enjoyed singing when I was at parties or fooling around with my family and friends, so I hooked the iPod into the sound system and I was ready to see if I could actually make Maynard sing like Garth Brooks.

Instead of the normal abrupt ending I said, 'OK fine. I'm not letting you leave this stage without singing a song!' I started the Garth Brooks song and began, through Maynard, to sing in Garth's voice without moving my lips.

After the show almost every person in the crowd came up and said that it was one of the most amazing things they had ever seen and that I should incorporate more impressions through puppets into my act. I had already been thinking about doing just that, and was incredibly relieved to find that I could pull it off.

Soon after that I was performing at a fair close to Las Vegas in Logandale, Nevada, and decided that I needed to spend the money to see Danny Gans, a fellow impressionist, at the Mirage Casino in Vegas.

Tickets were around a hundred dollars, a small fortune for a guy like me, who was barely scraping by, performing on free stages at county fairs, but I talked to Melinda about it and she agreed that it would be money well spent.

I sat through his show and began to get more and more excited as I watched the crowd respond enthusiastically to his impressions, and I realized that I could do many of the impressions, as well as or better than he, without moving my lips.

I was ecstatic. I left the show on a high I had never before experienced, and I called Melinda and told her I had just spent the best hundred dollars of my life, and that I was going to be a major headliner in Vegas; one day I was going to be a star. I went back to my hotel room that night with visions of billboards and a pictures of myself on the marquee outside a major casino.

I knew that I had a lot of work to do but I had never been afraid of hard work. It was, after all, much more fun to do this than clean buildings and houses. I started to rewrite my entire show, having every character I did perform songs and impressions of the singers who made them famous. I immediately felt the difference in my career.

I had been a solo act for a couple of years and had received my share of compliments, with folks telling me that I was a very accomplished ventriloquist—but once I started doing the impressions, the sentiment changed from people telling me I was very good—to exclaiming that they had never seen anything like it and asking me how in the world I wasn't famous.

I responded that I was working at it and that I hoped it would happen soon. I also started to get standing ovations at every show I did, even when the audience was small, although I was getting larger crowds than ever before.

I had done several fair showcases since I had struck out on my own, but the first year I incorporated impressions into my act I was performing at the Rocky Mountain Fair Association meeting. I was doing a showcase I had done for years, but this time my puppets did impressions of singers. I ended with my signature routine, 'What a Wonderful World' as sung by Louis Armstrong, and I did the voice flawlessly without a puppet.

The audience was thunderstruck! They leapt to their feet and I received one of the best standing ovations I've ever had, and afterwards I noticed that I was being treated differently that I had ever been, with one fellow entertainer after another treating me like a close friend—some of whom I hardly knew.

I called Melinda that night and laughed about it, telling her I thought everyone at that showcase knew I was going to be a big star and was hoping to cement themselves in my life as a friend before the fact, and I hoped they were right.

I was working more than I ever had, and having a great time at it—even though I was usually very tired. It was a good kind of tired though, in the way a day at Disneyland makes you worn-out, but it was an exhilarating exhaustion.

I had incorporated my impressions into all of my shows, including my school performances. It was so much fun, knowing that the unsuspecting audience would think they were about to see a normal ventriloquist, and leave saying that they had never experienced anything like it.

Part of me loved the surprise, but a bigger part of me longed for my audiences to come along, expecting to see something remarkable. The reason for this is that I had to spend so much of my energy convincing my audiences that they would enjoy it, so the first quarter of my show I had to expend most of my energy trying to keep folks from walking out. The exception to this was the elementary schools I played. The younger children, bless them, were mine the moment they saw a puppet.

Everyone else, however, was not so accepting. I had to work extra hard to prove to every other audience that they would love the show. Invariably I won them over, but it was an exhausting effort.

I experienced this exact prejudice against ventriloquists on the first episode of *America's Got Talent*. I walked onto the stage with the girl puppet I had named Emma Taylor and as soon as we appeared, David Hasselhoff leaned over to Sharon Osbourne and said, 'Oh no, a ventriloquist!'

I have had several people tell me they were very upset by his comment but I wasn't. I knew I had them right where I wanted them. My only fear was that they would buzz me with three Xs before I had the chance to have Emma sing, but I didn't have anything to worry about.

As expected and had happened countless times since I had started to do impressions in my show, the judges were blown away when Emma belted out 'At Last', in a perfect Etta James impression.

Emma Taylor was a gift from Melinda and my closest and dearest friends, Darrell and Sissy Johnson, the year I started doing the impressions. We had been together for Christmas and they gave Emma to me, saying that I didn't have any girl puppets to sing female songs and they hoped she would be useful. None of us had any idea how important she would become to my career.

I began to look at all the female vocalists I might be able to incorporate, and I thought about the song *At Last* by Etta James. I downloaded the song into my iPod and listened to it carefully. I found I was able to do a reasonably good impression of it, but not without moving my lips. I thought that it would be ridiculous for me to try to do the song without having a girl puppet do it, so I hunkered down and started working on it. After several days I was able to recreate Etta James' voice almost perfectly without moving my lips—so I started working with the new girl puppet.

She didn't have a name yet, so I held her up and started making her talk. I gave her a voice and began to have a little conversation with her. I asked her to tell me her name, and for some reason the name 'Emma Taylor' popped into my head, so she of course repeated it. I liked the sound of it, and Emma Taylor was born.

I asked Emma if she could do an impression of Etta James and she replied that she could. She opened her mouth wide and belted out 'AAAAAT LAAAAAASSTT!' and I knew I had a hit on my hands.

The next show I did I introduced my audience to Emma, asking her the same way I had so many times while rehearsing if she could do any impressions of singers. She said she could and I asked who she could do.

'You'll see!' she exclaimed.

The audience tittered, amused at the thought that my puppet knew what she would sing, but I didn't. (Actually that idea was Melinda's. I did the routine for her before I put it in my act and she suggested that Emma not tell me who she was going to do. As so often happens in my routines, my best stuff comes from Melinda!)

I watched the audience react when Emma uttered those two words, and their jaws literally dropped open in amazement, and afterwards they would come up to me and ask how it was possible that I could sing Etta James without moving my lips. I had no idea, but I was glad I could. Lots of people accused me of lip-synching and saying that what I do is impossible, but I really do sing everything live in my show, with the exception of the one Ashley Simpson joke where Emma lip-synchs to one of her songs and exclaims, 'That's what *she* does,' in reference to her infamous lip-synching gaff on *Saturday Night Live*.

I had finally found my niche, a ventriloquist who does impressions of singers through puppets, and I was having more fun than I ever had.

I could hardly wait until the end of my show when Emma would take the stage, and as soon as she started singing 'At Last' the audience would go crazy. I ended with 'What a Wonderful World', singing by myself as Louis Armstrong, and as soon as the show ended the crowd would leap to their feet and applaud enthusiastically, some with tears in their eyes from the emotions of hearing many of their long-dead favorite singers revived for the night through those charming little puppets.

I continued to work full-time as a ventriloquist/ impressionist and was starting to get more work doing corporate shows for more money. I was still unable to get anyone's attention to help me break into national recognition.

Every month or so I would send a video tape and DVD to Jay Leno and David Letterman imploring them to give me a chance, but every attempt met with rejection. I would watch in frustration as David Letterman started 'Ventriloquist Week' and would put a different one on every night. I was happy to see other ventriloquists getting air time, but I was deeply discouraged that I could not seem to get anyone to pay attention to my new act. I just *knew* that I would be a hit if only someone would notice me.

After a couple of years of slowly crawling my way up the ladder of corporate entertainment and fairs (I was getting more money than I ever had, although it was still not much, it was at least paying the bills) I heard about this new show Simon Cowell had created called *America's Got Talent*, to be aired on NBC.

Melinda asked me if I would be interested, but I said absolutely not. I just couldn't see myself doing a reality program. I did, of course, watch the show that season. I was amazed at how entertaining it was, and, lo and behold, there was a ventriloquist on it as well. His name was Kevin Johnson; he was quite good and even though he only made it through two episodes, I was being approached by people at every single gig I did, asking me if I had seen him on the show. Obviously it had a very wide audience and I considered that I might actually be interested in auditioning for the second season.

When I watched the next 'Ventriloquist Week' on David Letterman, lo and behold, Kevin Johnson was one of the ventriloquists he featured.

That settled it; I was going to audition for *America's Got Talent*. You see, since I was in college in 1983 I had dreamed of being on David Letterman.

I have explained earlier how strict my college was, and owning a television was forbidden by the laws of the school. Of course, I was Terry. (Please don't think I always had a casual disregard of all rules. I just didn't like silly ones that no one could defend. I was, after all, eighteen years old and felt that I ought to be able to watch television when I wanted, especially since my father had limited it so much growing up.) I knew I would find a way around that particular rule, so I went to a flea market and bought a little portable black and white television set, smuggled it into my dorm room and hid it in the ceiling tiles so it would never be found. True enough, no amount of surprise searches by the RAs (they were convinced I had a TV) turned up the much sought-after television set. Lights out was at 11pm and bed check was around 11.15pm so I had fifteen minutes to get the television out of the ceiling, turn it on, let it warm up and turn on the *Late Show with David Letterman*.

Jep still recalls many a night when he would sneak over to my room and we'd watch it together. I would watch in rapt attention, longing to be a Letterman guest myself, dreaming of the day I'd finally be able to appear and show off my talent.

So here was Kevin Johnson, doing Letterman like I had dreamed of for so many years, and it had all happened because of that little talent show on NBC.

I contacted the producers of *America's Got Talent* and asked for a schedule of auditions. It was September, 2006, and I was able to procure an audition while I was in Los Angeles after a day of playing schools in the area. (The auditions were for the producers to determine if one is good or bad enough to audition before the celebrity judges on television.)

I parked at the Los Angeles Convention Center and trudged up the walkways with my suitcase full of characters to the lobby where they were registering potential contestants, signed all the necessary paperwork, took a number and waited.

There were an awful lot of weirdos running around in various attire, each trying to stand out a little more than everyone else, as well as many singers and dancers who were rehearsing their routines intently while we all waited for the fateful sound of our name being called.

I wasn't really nervous as I waited. I had been doing the impressions and ventriloquism bits pretty much every night for two years at corporate events, schools and fairs all over the country, so I knew I was well prepared for the audition.

I wondered what it would be like inside the little rooms that people would go into, and either come out in tears from rejection—or elated at the news that they would be allowed to audition before the celebrity judges.

Finally they called out my name and I dragged my suitcase into the small room where five people were sitting at a table, one of which had a video camera pointed at me. I was wearing a suit I had purchased at Men's Wearhouse a few days earlier for this very audition and I thought I looked pretty good, even though it was one of the cheapest suits they sold. Hey, it was all I could afford. I pulled out a little battery-powered set of speakers, hooked my iPod into it, and then set out the puppets in the order in which I was going to perform with them.

I had edited a medley of the impressions I was going to do. I would have Walter T. Airdale sing a couple of country songs (Garth Brooks' 'Friends in Low Places' and Brooks and Dunn's 'Boot Scootin' Boogie') then I had Kermit sing 'Rainbow Connection', pulled out a Frank Sinatra puppet I had given the moniker Sammy Martin Sinatra (as a nod to the Rat Pack), had him sing Tony Bennett's 'I Left My Heart in San Francisco', had Emma Taylor sing 'At Last', then ended with Kermit and me singing 'What a Wonderful World' as a duet, with Kermit as himself and me as Louis Armstrong.

The producers were absolutely stunned. One of them said, 'That's ridiculous. You can't really be doing that. Where is the tape recorder hidden?'

I assured them there was no tape recorder and that I had done all of the voices live. They then made me come right up to the table and sing *At Last* about two feet from them so I could prove it really had been me singing.

Again they were absolutely amazed at my ability to sing like Etta James. They thanked me for my time and sent me downstairs. I left the small room and headed down the escalators to the room they had indicated, and as I walked in, the lady who was the security guard asked, 'Are you the guy who can sing like Etta James?' I replied that I was, and she asked me to do it, to which I cheerfully complied.

I told her I had been asked to do an interview down here and she said, 'Good for you. That means you are either really good or really bad!'

Smiling, I said, 'Well I know I'm not really bad.'

'Then congratulations!' came her retort.

I spent the next couple of hours watching the others who had been asked to do interviews, trying to direct attention from the video cameras at themselves by practicing their acts full voice and as loud as they could. Many would situate themselves directly behind the cameras as they would be interviewing another contestant, then start playing guitar and singing at the top of their voices so they would be heard during the other person's interview.

I sat quietly by myself and shook my head. This was the kind of stuff I knew had to be a part of the show that had kept me from auditioning the previous year.

I pulled out my Nintendo DS and quietly played a video game to get my mind off everything (I typically do that to relax myself in tense situations) until they called out my name for the interview.

Apparently I had become quite the sensation in the short time I had been waiting, since the producers I had auditioned for had radioed to everyone about my Etta James impression. All of the folks who worked there gathered around the cameras as they asked me to sing *At Last*, and everyone cheered afterwards.

I left the audition on a high and called Melinda to tell her it was almost a guarantee that I would do the show the next season. I finally had my chance at fame and fortune, as Etta James would say, 'At Last!'

Unbeknownst to me, the most difficult times of my professional career were right around the corner, and I almost gave it all up from frustration.

Chapter 8
Turbulence Ahead

From the moment I had done the audition for the producers, I began to feel an excitement about my future as an entertainer. I gave myself absolutely no chance at all of winning, but I felt that it would raise people's awareness of who I was so I could make more money doing corporate shows, schools and fairs.

My belief that I couldn't win *America's Got Talent* stemmed from the overall feeling from most that ventriloquism was a joke and that it was the lower of the art forms, just above mimes in the hierarchy of artistic endeavors. I honestly felt I had the talent to win it, but I knew I was up against a prejudice that was embedded in most of American society. I wasn't sure if Americans would be willing to curb the intense feeling that all ventriloquists were hacks who might be able to entertain young children but had no place in the adult entertainment arena. My only chance would be if folks realized that I was doing something completely different and that while I *was* a ventriloquist, I was so much more at the same time.

I began to work on my act in earnest, and doubled my efforts to perfect my technique while doing my regular performances. I would announce to every audience that I might be on *America's Got Talent* the following season, and to make sure and watch for it.

The months dragged on as I heard no word, and I began to feel a little disheartened about it. I had been told that the show would air in the spring, and by February I was downright depressed.

I assumed that I had been turned down, and that my life would continue as it had for the past twenty-five years, able to do what I loved but never getting the opportunity to allow millions to enjoy my efforts.

My true desire was to be able to get large audiences together to enjoy the routines I had written, instead of playing free stages at fairs and gathering twenty or so people together. Sure, they all came up afterwards to tell me they loved my stuff and to ask me why I wasn't famous, but it was very disheartening to know that I still had to work hard to keep every audience from walking out at the beginning.

I longed for the day when I could fill a hall and have everyone in the audience anxiously awaiting the show, excitedly discussing what they were about to see, and I would walk on stage to thunderous applause, and not have to prove anything to anyone, just do what I loved, what I had spent countless thousands of hours rehearsing for the benefit of all those who had bought a ticket to see me.

As I have said, by February I was down in the dumps about it all, but an agent had booked a show that might be my big break.

I had spent a lifetime thinking that the next big chance was the one, and I never gave up that hopeless optimism. Melinda had given up hoping that every one of those opportunities would lead to success. She knew that I had it in me and told me so, but we had so often had our hopes and dreams dashed to the ground, she just kept saying, 'When it happens, it happens. I'm tired of getting my hopes up and being disappointed time and again.'

I'm Terry, though. Every opportunity was the one that was finally going to convince the world I belonged alongside the greats, such as Edgar Bergen, Paul Winchell, and Shari Lewis.

That February (2007) I had been booked for a corporate event at Rio in Las Vegas, and my agent had called three top Vegas producers to come and see me, and let us know if I had what it took to play Vegas.

I took the stage and did my best show, ending with Kermit the Frog singing his duet of 'What a Wonderful World' with me doing my Louis Armstrong.

The audience leapt to their collective feet and the applause was deafening.

I went over to the table where the producers sat, thinking they'd be nuts to turn me down and just knew that this was it!

Each of them, one by one, explained that I just wasn't Vegas material and would probably never be able to maintain a show here. The last one told me I wasn't good-looking enough to be a Vegas headliner. That remark stung because I have always been very self-conscious about my looks. My father had repeatedly told me I was a very average-looking guy and shouldn't expect girls to like me much.

This feeling was compacted by an incident when I was with TEXAS the band. I had just finished a set and a woman came up to me, hardly able to contain her laughter and told me I reminded her of Jon Lovitz in *The Wedding Singer*, a character that was a ridiculous caricature of an ugly guy who thought he was sexy. To this day I cannot think of myself as sexy except as a joke.

I told Melinda and Debi about what that lady told me and they laughed, saying it was ridiculous and that I shouldn't care, but here was this Vegas producer telling me I wasn't good-looking enough to headline Vegas.

I was very disheartened once again, resigning myself to a life of professional obscurity.

As difficult as it was to realize that I would never be able to reach most of my dreams and goals, I had come to the conclusion several years earlier that I was not going to work only because of the hope of fame and fortune; no, I was going to work for my own sake. I decided that even if I never got the popularity I craved, I would still be the best I could be and make sure that everyone who came to see me left feeling that they had been a part of the best show in the world.

I worked harder than ever to make sure that I never got sloppy on stage and that my technique was world class.

Even though I realized that I had very little chance of ever becoming famous I began to carry a Sharpie pen in my pocket and say to myself, 'One day I will need this because people will want my autograph.'

I think my career reached its low point in April of 2005 when I was performing at a fair in Texas, and around my scheduled time to perform it started raining, which made things impossible because my stage was outside as most of my fair shows were. Most fairs scheduled me for afternoon performances, which drove me crazy because it never gave me an opportunity to build a fan base. I felt I was good enough to appear on the real stages in the evening, but almost no fair I played agreed, and stuck me on the awful stages when very few people were even at the fair.

I played them all faithfully, and rarely complained to anyone except Melinda and Debi, but they always gave me wonderful encouragement and helped me to keep plugging away.

All of the difficult times at fairs culminated at this particular one in Texas when it started to rain.

I am not one to try to find ways to cancel. I have never missed a performance that I did not do a make-up show for, and I am very proud to have that track record. While many fair entertainers would look for an excuse to get out of a show, I went to the fair office and told them that it was raining and that I needed an indoor facility to perform in.

They told me there was a small theater on the grounds that held about a thousand people and that I could set up in it and they would announce over the loudspeaker that I would be doing a show there.

Debi was with me that night and was running my merchandise booth. I set up for the show and waited for the audience to arrive.

Only one person, a twelve-year-old boy, turned up.

About ten minutes in, three teenagers came in and sat down, and I joked that we might actually be getting an audience.

My hopes were dashed when a couple of minutes later a man arrived and told the teenagers to get to work; they were the custodial staff and started to fold up the chairs in the theater. Debi howled with laughter, and again, it was a funny moment and I laughed as well, but I felt as low as I ever had in my entire career. I commented that it looked like the show was over and I went out and met the kid and gave him a set of my merchandise (a home-made DVD and a CD of my original tunes) and thanked him for coming.

Now I don't want you to think Debi was being cruel to laugh. It was a funny situation, but also very humiliating. Debi told me afterwards that she thought it would be a great story to tell once I got famous and was on television and she was right. *America's Got Talent* told that story and all of America sympathized with me so it was worth it all, but it was still a hard pill to swallow that day.

I got to the hotel room that night and I called Melinda, feeling despondent about my career. I told her I was ready to call it quits. I had not heard from *America's Got Talent*, I had been rejected by Vegas, and it truly seemed that no matter how hard I worked I would never be able to make my mark on the world of entertainment.

Melinda said, 'Did they pay you?'

Surprised, I answered, 'Well, yeah, they did.'

'Then stop complaining. One day someone who can help you is going to see how amazing you are as an entertainer and you will set the world on fire. It *will* happen, and until it does, at least you are making a paycheck.'

What a woman! She hates it when I tell that story because she thinks everyone will think she is money-grubbing, but I love the story since it reminded me that I did get to do what I loved even though sometimes it was a struggle, and I even got paid to do it.

That event made me really think about the millions of people who don't have the luxury of a job doing something they love, and it gave me a whole new perspective and a second wind. From then on, any time something happened that upset me at a show, I happily thought about the paycheck I would receive and I thanked God for giving me the talent to do such a wonderful job *and* get paid to do it.

I had a whole new perspective on my future, but things were about to change, because a few short days after that terrible show I came home and there was a message on my answering machine from Elyse Foley, one of the producers I had auditioned for from *America's Got Talent*. She had called to excitedly inform me that I would be auditioning before the celebrity judges at the end of April.

I was elated! Melinda and I were jumping around and I kept shouting, 'This could be it! I think I might become a star, Melinda!' And I hugged her tight.

We stood in our living room in front of the answering machine and held each other for a few moments before she said, 'You know me, honey. I don't want to get my hopes up. We have thought too many times that your big chance had arrived. But one thing I do know. America is going to finally see the best ventriloquist in the world and I can't wait!'

But you know me. I went to sleep that night dreaming of the day I would finally be able to present my hard efforts to David, Sharon, and Piers, as well as all of America.

This is it! I thought as I drifted off to sleep. *I'm gonna be a star!*

Chapter 9

Yes, Virginia, America *Does* Have Talent

As I stepped out of the car to say goodbye to Melinda at DFW Airport, a sense of excitement welled up inside me that I had never felt before.

I was finally off to the real *America's Got Talent* auditions, and Melinda got out of the car and hugged me tightly. 'Good luck,' she whispered.

'Thanks,' I replied quietly.

We kissed and I made my way into the terminal, the prospect of the future dancing about in my head like dandelion seeds flitting about on a warm summer afternoon.

I checked into my flight with the delightful surprise that Mel had upgraded me to first class. I called to thank her and she said that I was going off to become a star and that I needed to fly in like one. She's so sweet.

The flight was an exciting one, with visions of what it would be like to perform on national television for the first time in my life crowding my thoughts. I wasn't nervous, just very excited. The plane landed in Burbank and I went to baggage claim to collect my luggage, mostly puppets, and one bag for my clothes and get-ready stuff. I got my bags and spotted a guy holding a sign that said 'America's Got Talent: Season 2' in large letters.

I meandered over to him and shyly introduced myself and asked where I needed to go. He pointed to the place where other contestants were waiting and I went over and stood patiently with them as the rest of the contestants scheduled to be picked up by my bus arrived.

We loaded on and I sat down, excitedly taking in the feelings of anticipation we all must have been feeling. I remember distinctly thinking that the winner of this year's contest might very well be on this bus!

I looked closely at everyone, including a couple who did tricks on unicycles, and a pretty girl who called herself 'Butterscotch', who I later misidentified as 'Buttercup'. She politely corrected me, much to my embarrassment.

Never one to be quiet, I engaged in conversation with anyone who would talk to me, asking about particular talents and the hopes of my fellow riders.

It was the same story for all of us. We were here in the hope that our fortunes would change and that we could move into a different level of the entertainment field. Some had more of a shot than others. There were those of us who had dedicated ourselves to our craft for years, and others who were relatively new at their abilities and hoped to find a short cut to fame and fortune—but the one thing that bonded us all was our desire to reach that next elusive level in our respective careers.

The bus ride was a short one, and since the interviews had already begun we didn't have time to go by the hotel and drop our stuff off.

We filed into the studio in Burbank and were escorted into an elevator that took us down into the basement of the television studio.

The room we all gathered in, and in which I would spend much of the upcoming summer, became affectionately known as 'The Dungeon'. It wasn't much more than a large room consisting of concrete walls painted white. There were two rooms like that, except that one of them had some curtains dividing up the room, so contestants would have a little privacy to change their clothes.

I arrived to the room filled with people and I sat back in silence as I drank it all in. People were chatting, and there were some cold-cut sandwiches and potato chips, as well as some candy and coffee sitting on a table at the far end. Since I hadn't eaten anything, I was famished. I grabbed a ham sandwich, a bag of chips, and a soda and sat on the floor to eat and watch the floor show, the craziest group of humans I had ever seen gathered in one place.

There were girls dressed in feathery outfits practicing dance routines, and an enormous black man donning a tight leather outfit and covered in piercings and tattoos, accompanied by an equally massive man holding a guitar. They would periodically break into song, trying to drown out the sounds of a hundred other hopefuls attempting to get a little camera attention as well. There were young girls dressed to the nines in little Irish dancing outfits and they were tap-tap-tapping away, much to the delight of the small crowd who had gathered to watch them rehearse.

After a few minutes of silently watching this nuttiness unfold, I observed Jerry Springer walking into the room followed by a camera crew. They filmed him as he interviewed several of the contestants, and even after the cameras were turned off, Jerry continued to voice encouragement to the eager star-seekers.

I was struck by just how down-to-earth and kind Jerry Springer was. I admit that I was a little disappointed to find out that the second season of *America's Got Talent* would not have Regis Philbin hosting, but after I met Jerry I really liked him and he always made everyone feel special, no matter how ridiculous their supposed 'talent' was—and I ended up very happy, feeling that he was and is the right man for the job.

I met some very nice people that day, including twin sisters who have a dueling piano show in Las Vegas, and a concert pianist. We sat around and talked of our hopes and dreams and what we expected from this opportunity to have national exposure.

I had decided early on that I was not going to try to create a persona for the TV cameras. I was going to just expose my real self to America and if they liked me, great; if not, at least I would have been honest. I never prepared my answers or thought about what I was going to say. I just bared my soul and hoped for the best. The cameras finally trained on me and I was asked several questions about my life and career. I answered as honestly as I could and when it was over I was told to go back to the bus which would take us to the Sheraton Universal Hotel to check in.

In the lobby I met a very nice guy named Cas Haley and we talked about both being from Texas and hit it off immediately. Unbeknownst to us we were to spend much of our time together for the next several months, but at that moment we just shared the excitement of the audition before David Hasselhoff, Sharon Osbourne, and Piers Morgan.

The shooting was to begin at around 8am the next morning, so I called and babbled on excitedly to Melinda for a while before trying to calm myself enough to get some sleep. I was unsuccessful, and spent the entire night fantasizing of being on a national television show and what it could potentially lead to in my life and career.

I was up three hours too early and went down to eat a casual breakfast and drink a cup of coffee and to try and relax, again to no avail. I just couldn't stop my brain from racing from one thing to another. This could be it! The moment I had dreamed of, and prayed for, and longed for since I was a child.

Fleetingly, I wondered if my father would watch me, but the thought was gone as quickly as it had come. I wasn't about to let that crazy idea distract me, not now, not in my moment of truth.

Finally the bus arrived and I got on with my suitcase holding Emma Taylor, the puppet I would make my television debut with.

I had struggled to know what to do for the first televised audition. I had worked for over twenty years to develop many wonderful routines and characters, and over the past two years I had perfected many impressions with fabulous puppets. My dilemma was very different from most of the other contestants trying out. Most of them had to figure out exactly what they would do week to week, but I had so much good material I had to decide which ones to *not* do!

My first impulse was to save the most amazing impression, that of Etta James singing 'At Last' through my puppet Emma Taylor, until a later episode, but I came to the conclusion that since the show is one of elimination, I had better not try to save anything on the hope I would be back. I made the decision that, week after week, I would put forth the absolute best I had to offer, and then try to top it the next week, if I was fortunate enough to continue.

So here I was, boarding the bus with Emma in hand and a heart full of hope and anticipation.

We got to the studio and were once again escorted to The Dungeon, where we waited for our names to be called.

The atmosphere was much more subdued than the day before, as all of us knew that the big moment was at hand, but many were still trying to get in a last rehearsal or two, before the fateful call to action.

As I sat and waited, one after another of the contestants would be called, leave the room for a half hour or so, and return to The Dungeon in tears or fury, weeping or shouting about how the judges were so unfair and hadn't even given them the chance to finish their routine. This happened with such alarming regularity that I began to panic.

Oh, my Lord, what have I gotten myself into? I thought. *This might have been a HUGE mistake!*

My one fear was that the judges would immediately give me three Xs as soon as they saw the puppet and not even give me the chance to perform. I knew that the feelings about ventriloquists were not terribly positive, mainly due to the fact that most ventriloquists we see are not very good.

Finally my name was called and I headed up to the backstage area to await my audition.

I had been a professional entertainer for more than two decades, and had not felt a nervous knot in my stomach for many years, but as I waited to go on stage I felt the cocoons that had obviously been waiting to open in my stomach let the butterflies loose with a vengeance.

I swallowed hard and heard my name. I strode on stage looking much more confident than I felt and stood before the judges. I couldn't hear what David Hasselhoff said to Sharon Osbourne, but I could definitely feel the eye-rolling and the air of, 'Oh, no, not this!'

Later, when the show aired on TV, I heard David say, 'Oh, no! A ventriloquist!'

What they didn't know was that this was the reaction I had hoped for. I knew that if I could lull them into a false sense of low expectations they would be mine as soon as Emma belted out those fateful words "AAAAT LAAAAAAST!"

Thankfully they did actually let me start, and as the music started to play I asked Emma what she was doing. 'You'll see,' she replied. The audience laughed.

'Do you know who this is?' I protested.

'Yep,' She replied.

'You're going to do an impression of her?' I asked incredulously.

'Yeah!' she fired back.

The audience continued to laugh; amused by the fact that Emma seemed to be out of my control.

And then it happened. Emma started to sing and David and Sharon leapt to their feet in shock. The audience soon followed suit. Three times during my short ninety-second audition the audience leapt to their collective feet to cheer Emma and her amazing voice.

The judges raved about my performance calling me 'quite brilliant', and Piers said he had never before seen a ventriloquist do impressions of singers, and it was 'quite amazing.' David said I had a long way to go to win the million dollars, but that I had made a great start.

I had made it to the Las Vegas audition! We would be taping it in a couple of weeks at Planet Hollywood, and I left the stage feeling a satisfaction I had never before experienced in my professional life.

I was through the first audition and was continuing on.

I had no delusion that I would win the show; I knew that the prejudice most people felt toward ventriloquism would probably be far too strong for me to actually be voted the most talented act in the country; I was just happy to be moving forward. That meant I would be on TV twice instead of just once, and any exposure I could get was worth far more than any money I might win. I just wanted to make sure I never had to do another show for one kid again. I was hoping to gain enough of a name to pull in crowds whenever I performed, which was all I wanted or expected from my appearance on *America's Got Talent*.

I only had to wait a couple of weeks before the Las Vegas audition took place, and it went by quickly.

My secret fear was that the world would find out that my father's continuous declaration to me as I grew up was true. He had consistently told me that I wasn't really talented, merely good at fooling people into thinking I was talented.

I'm not exactly sure what the difference is, but it seemed real enough to me as I worked on my career throughout the years. I always felt that my entire profession was built on a house of cards and that as soon as people wised up, it would all come crashing down around me. Secretly I hoped I could make it through the show and fool America that I really did have talent. I would worry about keeping up the (supposed) façade after it was over.

It sounds so silly now that I write this all down. It is simply amazing to me how much influence the idiotic words of a person (like a father) can have on the children involved. If there are any parents out there reading this, I hope you take to heart how your words can affect your children, even though they may be unintended.

I made the trip to Vegas along with all of the other contestants from around the country, and the whirlwind started immediately. As soon as I stepped off the bus from the airport I was greeted by one of the producers.

'Terry Fator? Come this way. We have a special shoot for you at the spa.'

I followed dutifully and was led to the spa where a bath was already drawn, and the producer told me to get a puppet out and ready and to take my clothes off and get into the tub.

Sounds nice, doesn't it? A nice hot bubble bath after a long flight. The trouble was that the bath had been drawn long before I had arrived and the water was freezing cold. They added more water to make sure the bubbles stayed, but I not only had to strip with the camera crew around, I had to sit in the freezing water under the bubbles until the shoot was done, which consisted of me receiving a drink with an umbrella in it from the spa staff as I said, 'This is the life', as the camera panned over to Emma on a massage table.

All in all it was fun if a little uncomfortable, and I was happy to be getting a little extra camera time.

We got up the next morning and met in the large convention room. We had a special guest speaker (the creator of the Blue Man Group) and he told us what to expect. He said that when all the fun was over, if we won this competition we must plan on working harder than we had ever dreamed —but that the journey and work would all be worth it.

As I sat surrounded by the other contestants, all of us hopeful and full of dreams of stardom and fortune, I looked around, wondering which of these people would be the one to have their lives changed forever, never even entertaining the idea that it would be me.

My attitude from the beginning was that I just wanted to get through one more episode. I would be happy if I could get that little bit more television exposure. I never looked beyond the next episode. I always expected to be kicked off in the next round so I focused on making every round count. I had decided to take advantage of the three minutes they were giving each of us in Vegas to do a medley of songs, including the duet 'Unforgettable', with me singing Nat King Cole's part and Emma singing Natalie Cole's. I

then brought out a Frank Sinatra character and had him sing
'That's Amore' as Dean Martin, and 'I Left my Heart In
San Francisco' as Tony Bennett. I spent several hours a day
rehearsing my routines in my room, and the rest of the time
we were getting organized and learning the schedule—when
we would be actually performing, when lunch and dinner
breaks would be, and so forth.

The excitement was palpable as hundreds of us hopefuls
all spent so much time in the main hall waiting for the real
deal to come down. I sought out new friends and discussed
strategies with them. I was delighted to meet Luigi, who
went by the name Boy Shakira. He had an odd little act in
which he dressed in revealing attire like Shakira and did a
belly dance. He was mostly alone, so I befriended him and
made sure he always had someone to talk to, as well as eat
lunch and dinner with, and we enjoyed our time together.

As I had throughout my life, I sought out the ones who
looked lonely, and spent my time with them. What's the
point of trying to hang out with folks who already have a lot
of attention around them? I had a very rewarding time with
Luigi and a few others I met during my stay in Vegas.

The reason we were here, though, was not to socialize but
to perform, and the day finally arrived when we all had to
gather in the taping room.

Simon Cowell got up and gave us a pep talk, telling us
that we had the opportunity to turn it up and impress the
judges and that we should take advantage of it as best as
we could. The judges each made a speech of their own,
with David Hasselhoff inviting us to soda and burgers at his
house, joking about a recently released embarrassing video
that had just made the rounds of him drunk, eating a burger
on the floor of his hotel room. I admired his ability to be
light about it and thought how difficult it must be to have a

fault splayed before the whole world, as if somehow being a celebrity makes one immune to human shortcomings.

The anticipation began to build as the producers told us how we were to be separated into singers and musical acts and variety acts.

The audience was to consist of our fellow contestants, and I must say it was a lot of fun and all of the contestants showed wonderful support to their fellow competitors.

During this round the judges were not going to comment after each individual performance; instead they would give us our evaluation when they told us the news of whether we would be going back to LA to compete in the top twenty contestants.

The shows were a lot of fun, some quite bizarre, but we all gave it everything we had and at the end of the two days most of us felt that we had a great chance of moving forward.

My audition went flawlessly and I got a standing ovation from the crowd. I felt good about my chances, but I also knew that the judges could be very unpredictable. In spite of the fact that almost every other contestant assured me I would make it into the top twenty, I never count my chickens before they hatch, and my stomach was in knots when the night finally arrived to find out our fate: would we be going home disappointed or would our dream continue on?

I had the sinking feeling that this was my last real shot. I knew in my heart that if I failed to make an impact this time around I would never get an opportunity like this again.

I had thought several times during the previous few years that America is just not going to give much thought to a forty-year-old ventriloquist and I longed desperately to make the most of this, my final real shot to make my mark on the entertainment world.

I confided these feelings to Melinda, and although she didn't share my negative assessment (she said, 'If you don't get discovered here, someone else will find you. You're too good to not get discovered some day!') she knew that it was do or die, at least for this season of *America's Got Talent*.

I nervously awaited my name to be called. The cameras were rolling and one after another the contestants would leave the waiting area and emerge either in tears or celebrating. Which would it be for me?

My name was called and I vaguely remember someone saying that there was a red line I needed to stay on. 'Just walk up to the judges' table and stop at the microphone. On your way back make sure to follow the red line again.'

As if I were in a dream, time slowed down as I approached the judges' table.

I remember them talking about how difficult it is in these situations to cull down so much talent to only twenty acts and that their job was extremely difficult. I wasn't sure if they were toying with me or if I was about to receive the axe.

Piers told me that my talent was quite unusual and asked how long I had done it. I told him that I had been a ventriloquist since childhood but I had started to do the impressions and ventriloquism together two years before, at the suggestion of my agent.

David asked if my agent was there in Vegas and I replied that he wasn't.

'Well, you'll have to get him a plane ticket to LA because you made the top twenty!'

All three of the judges began to talk animatedly and raving about how amazing my talent was and that they had never seen anything like it. I didn't hear much of what was said because as soon as David told me I had made the top twenty, my body started to vibrate from the top of my head and it quickly spread down all the way to my feet. I could literally feel my body quiver all over. I actually felt as though I was floating as I tried to remember to stay on the red line all the way back to the backstage area.

The cameras were shoved in my face (to my delight) and I babbled something of which I have no recollection, and Jerry Springer asked me how it felt to know I would be continuing on. My eyes welled up with tears as I told him I had worked and struggled for more than twenty years and that I was finally seeing my dreams come true. Emotion took over as I hugged those backstage and tried to console those whose dreams had ended, if only temporarily. It is very hard for me to feel others' despair in moments like that because I had had my dreams dashed so many times and I had always looked at every failure as just another step to success. I even remember thinking as I saw one after another kicked-off contestants acting as though their dreams had been destroyed, *There is always another opportunity out there! Just keep striving!* Still, I tried to console them as best I could.

But my path in this particular endeavor was not over. I would fly to LA to shoot more of the show, and now I didn't have the unpredictable equation of the judges' whims. I would be allowed to let America decide if they liked my talent or not, and I must say I felt a great sense of relief.

My plan was to try to get the attention of America, so that they sat at home and said, 'OK that was interesting. But what can he do as an encore?'

I wanted people to anticipate the next puppet and impression, and I thought if I could accomplish that I might at least get on a couple of more episodes, and that meant more air time.

The wait before the next episode taping was excruciating.

We had more than a month before they were to continue taping, and we were instructed in no uncertain terms not to tell anyone, not even family members, that we had made it into the top twenty.

I did as they said. I was taking no chances at being disqualified, and the only person I told was Melinda. Not even my closest friends and family knew. It felt like being Superman and not being able to tell anyone. I love to talk, and to try to keep something that exciting to myself was pure hell for me.

I did somehow make it through, but the waiting game got ever more frustrating. No-one seemed to know when my first episode would be airing.

I had auditioned in Los Angeles but I was from Dallas, so I wasn't sure if they were going to air my first audition (with Emma singing 'At Last') in the Dallas or LA show. I told all of my friends and family to watch each week.

The LA audition came and went without me on it, so since the description said the next audition would be the Dallas one, I was absolutely convinced I would make my television debut that week. I excitedly told all of my friends and family to tune in, and several of them had watching parties, eagerly waiting for my national spotlight unveiling.

Again, the Dallas audition came and went and I wasn't on it. I was devastated. Had they decided to take me out of the show? What had happened?

I told all my friends and family that the Chicago auditions would be on the following week and to be sure and watch it just in case I was on it.

The week dragged on forever. I just couldn't stand waiting again and I prayed that it would be on that next week.

The producers of *America's Got Talent* had decided to air my audition during the Chicago auditions. I never found out why, but finally I was watching myself on TV with my friends, Darrell and Sissy, in their Austin house.

We were jumping up and down, hooting and hollering and toasting one another.

I was so proud! The judges had nothing but nice things to say except when David Hasselhoff said, 'Oh no, a ventriloquist!'

I had done it! I had been on TV! Now all I had to do was hang on until the Las Vegas episode aired and I could go to Burbank to continue taping.

The wait was excruciating. It was weeks before the Las Vegas episode aired, and I was terribly disappointed to find out that they had cut my entire performance and the only thing they showed was me in the hot tub being handed a drink. They also showed a very short clip of me getting through to the top twenty, and then it was over.

We were all stunned. That was it? A total of maybe forty-five seconds of air time? I felt so let down.

The only reason I was doing the show was to get the publicity to help my career, and now they had pretty much left me on the cutting-room floor.

Well, on the bright side, I could now talk to my family about the fact that I was in the top twenty of a national reality contest.

Also, Elyse called me and told me they wanted home video footage of the top twenty contestants, so I invited Cass Haley (he lived about a half-hour from my house) and his family over for a barbecue. We each performed a little and ate a good meal, laughing and talking all the while.

We videotaped it, and they ended up using footage of it throughout the entire run.

I can't remember how long it was before I flew to Burbank to continue the show, but I don't think it was very long.

I arrived at the Universal City Sheraton to find many of the wonderful people I had met previously, all of us excitedly babbling on about the different watch parties we had attended with our families and friends.

Cas and I caught up and we had dinner that night, along with several of the other top twenty contestants including Julienne Irwin and her father, Butterscotch, Boy Shakira, Kasheef, and Robert Hatcher.

We talked excitedly about the future and how it was going to be. All of us had the same dream: to win the show and be an instant millionaire, and hopefully famous as well.

There is nothing more enjoyable than sharing the excitement of a moment such as that with like-minded people, and we certainly did so that night.

The next morning we headed to the studio, where we spent the bulk of the day in The Dungeon, with short breaks to do interviews and have the producers tell us what to expect in the upcoming weeks.

I had decided that my first routine in the top twenty contest would have to be the one where I had Kermit the Frog sing a duet, with me doing my impression of Louis Armstrong singing 'What a Wonderful World'.

I submitted the routine for approval and got a call soon afterwards. The Muppets would not allow me to do Kermit on television. I was absolutely crushed. I had decided that the one routine I had that pretty much guaranteed people would want to see what I did the following week, and would therefore vote for me, was 'What a Wonderful World'.

I called Melinda in a panic. I told her I had no idea what to do now. How could I pull off the routine now that The Muppets had refused to let me do Kermit? (By the way, I was never upset with The Muppets for their decision. I completely understood their reasoning which is that every

Muppet should have one voice and one operator and this rule as such should never be broken. I was just very disappointed.)

Melinda and I discussed our options. I could choose another song, but I felt strongly that this was the one which would really wake up the public to the difference between me and your average ventriloquist.

We talked about different types of puppets. Perhaps I could get a different species (besides a frog) and have that puppet do an impression of Kermit just as I was doing an impression of Louis.

We went through several ideas before Melinda found a cute little turtle puppet online. I loved him and told her to order it and have it FedExed to the studios.

He arrived the next day and as I opened the box and saw him looking at me, I immediately knew his name and voice.

I picked him up out of his cardboard turtle carrier and put my hand inside his head and he said, 'Hello, I'm Winston the Impersonating Turtle.'

Everyone around giggled and remarked how very cute he was, and they were right: he was *extremely* cute!

I feel so fortunate that I was able to create his character so quickly, since it can sometimes take years in development.

I chose his name based on an experience I had at a Fourth of July picnic a couple of weeks prior. Melinda and I had spent the Fourth of July at the home of our cousins, Michael and Joy Blue, in East Texas.

They had a miniature donkey named Winston who thought he was a dog. He had been rejected by his mother because he was tiny, and Michael and Joy had taken him into the house and bottle-fed him—so he thought it was his home.

For some reason he really took to me that day and spent much of his time nuzzling up against me, begging me to pet him. I absolutely loved him and he made such an impact on me that I decided to give him his place in immortality by naming my new turtle puppet after him. Plus the new turtle *looked* like a Winston!

So now I had a puppet and a character to go along with it, as well as a song to sing. I was ready.

Melinda flew in to watch the taping and so did Debi, Jep, Melinda's mom and aunt, Shirley Walker and Joyce Blue, respectively.

I had also flown in a friend of mine, Christian rock legend Larry Norman, to see the first top twenty show live. Earlier that year Melinda had bought me a ticket to meet Larry on his sixieth birthday.

She had found out that Larry would be doing an historic concert on his birthday that consisted of him performing live every song in order from a trilogy of albums he is best known for. Mel paid $500 for me to be able to sit at the head table and meet Larry personally, and she knew that the money we paid was to help Larry with his considerable medical expenses because he had been in failing health for several years.

Even though we really couldn't afford it, I can never thank Melinda enough for that gift since it led to a very rewarding friendship with someone who had been a great influence in my early life; in fact, I would say that his music was one of the things that kept me going in the most difficult times in my youth, as I struggled with the difficulties of growing up in such a strained environment.

While contacting Kristen, the lady organizing Larry's birthday party, I casually mentioned to her that I was a ventriloquist. She responded by telling me that Larry was a huge fan of ventriloquism and had even tried it himself when he was young. She asked if I would perform at his birthday party and of course I said yes, since that was what I was hoping for all along.

I went to the concert, which was simply awesome, and being able to see Larry perform in a small room with only a hundred people or so, chatting between songs, was one of the most wonderful times I have ever had, and I will cherish it forever.

Larry was obviously in bad health and kept forgetting the words to his songs, which was charming and even more entertaining to me than to see a slickly produced show, and the next night we had his actual birthday party, at which I was scheduled to perform.

I did my best impressions, including Etta James, Garth Brooks and Tony Bennett, along with a few jokes I wrote for the occasion. At one point I said that Walter T. Airdale wanted to do an impression of Larry. He came out donned in a jet-black long wig, the exact opposite of Larry's actual hair, which had always been as blonde as can be, and I asked Walter about it. He replied that he was doing an impression of Larry before he got so old. Larry howled with laughter.

Walter started into a Larry Norman song, and a line or two into it forgot the words. I pointed it out and Walter said matter of factly, 'I know, I'm doing an impression of Larry from last night!'

Again, Larry doubled over with laughter. Much of the crowd didn't know how to react and watched Larry uncomfortably to make sure it was OK to laugh, but it was more than OK, Larry was in absolute hysterics.

Larry got up after my performance and raved about my fresh, original material and how, while most ventriloquists were corny, I had written jokes about the night before and things that had happened as early as that afternoon, and told the story of how when he was young he had received a ventriloquist puppet for his birthday and he had dreamed of one day becoming a ventriloquist himself, but that he had lacked the talent.

I sat and beamed, since here was one of my heroes complimenting me, and I have rarely been as proud as I was at that moment.

I remember thinking that even if my dad didn't think I was any good, at least Larry Norman did, and that meant more to me than a thousand compliments from my nutty father.

Anyway, I flew Larry and his son to the first top twenty performance and to my Las Vegas headliner debut, and we became close friends, talking on the phone as often as we could, and I cherished his opinions about how to improve my act.

Larry died in early 2008, and as much as I miss him I will forever be grateful that he told me I had provided him with one of the most fun years of his entire life by making him a part of my exciting times during those months.

After Larry's funeral I visited his family and they presented me with the actual ventriloquist puppet Larry had been given when he was five, along with a card thanking me for giving him such a great last year. I will cherish it forever.

⁓

Anyway, (again with the ADD and a new spin-off tale!) many family and friends came to that first top twenty taping.

Darrell and Sissy were there also, and as we were discussing making signs for my cheering section, Sissy came up with an absolutely brilliant idea. She suggested that my section wear sock puppets and hold them up as they were cheering me on.

I loved the idea and immediately called Debi, who is one of the most talented, artistic people I know. As usual in our family (thanks to our father) she has always struggled with thinking she was not very good at anything, in spite of the fact that her artistic creativity is astounding. I asked her if she could make about thirty sock puppets for my group, and as she always did in those situations, she came through in spades. She made up the cutest sock puppets anyone has ever seen and I distributed them to my family and friends.

The producers loved the idea and they got a lot of shots of the sock puppets during the taping.

I performed 'What a Wonderful World' with Winston and the judges raved, much to my relief. I was lauded by some as a sort of genius for coming up with the idea to have a turtle do an impression of a frog, but as you have all seen by this story, necessity is still the mother of invention.

I have to admit that when I first found out that The Muppet performers wouldn't let me do Kermit I was extremely disappointed. I even asked God what was going on. I had believed strongly He would work it out so I would be able to do my Kermit routine. I had even told Melinda that I just knew I would get permission, and I really did feel that I would.

Have you ever done that? You know, where you just had a palpable feeling that something was going to happen, and then had it all go wrong. That was how I felt. I was so sure I would get permission.

I'll admit that I was a little irritated with God for not coming through. Of course, as I found out later, His plan was so much better than I had originally thought, and I think Winston went over far better than even I anticipated, and he eventually ended up winning the whole shebang for me!

Maybe you think I'm a little bit nuts to think that God

even cares about who wins a competition like that, and you may be right. After all, what about all the other contestants who begged God to let them win and they didn't; but I like to think He does care; and just like me wanting so badly to be able to use a Kermit puppet in that first routine in spite of all my carefully-laid plans, God had a better plan for all of them as well. Maybe it's all just hogwash, and that's OK if it is, but I truly take comfort in the idea that He cares.

OK, this ADD thing is getting out of control. How the heck did I end up in a theological discussion while telling the story of a turtle puppet? The ADD-addled brain is a goofy thing, as my poor wife has discovered countless times during our marriage. I'll blurt something out that seems completely unrelated to anything we may have been discussing, and when she asks me how the heck I thought of that, I will go through this ridiculous train of thought about how I arrived at that particular subject.

OK, so now I had just finished the routine and the judges really liked it. Watching it later, my favorite part was when, as soon as Winston started singing, the judges, for a tiny moment, cocked their collective heads and had the most child-like expressions on their faces. You can see it on YouTube if you look for it.

I knew I had touched their souls when that happened.

America agreed, because I was voted on to the next round.

The first couple of rounds of the top twenty episodes were very difficult because there were so many acts, many of which consisted of several people. Getting fitted for costumes (thanks to Katja Cahill and Joy Freeman) and doing interviews was a nightmare and we waited around for hours at a time to get anything accomplished, but I never, ever complained.

I was asked by one of the crew of *America's Got Talent* why I never complained, and I replied that I had waited my whole life for this opportunity and I didn't care how difficult it was, I was going to cherish ever single moment. I stayed true to that feeling and never once griped about the difficult and grueling schedules.

My next job was to decide which routine to do next, and I felt that it was a good time to bring back Emma Taylor.

I had been doing a routine for several months in my live show where Emma and I sang 'Unforgettable' as Nat King Cole and Natalie Cole, and Emma would flirt with me during the song, nuzzling and biting my ear, and it always got lots of laughs and the audience seemed to enjoy it a lot, so I decided that that was going to be my next routine.

Again the judges loved it, and Piers said, 'Let's not beat about the bush, you are the best ventriloquist I have ever seen!' As he said it I remembered vividly thinking to myself when I was fourteen years old that I wanted to be known as the best ventriloquist in the world. I had just had one of the judges on a national television show proclaim that I was the best he had ever seen, and my body flushed with exhilaration as soon as he said it. Sharon exclaimed that she wasn't sure if people realized just how difficult what I was doing actually *was*. Melinda had expressed many times that I made it all look too easy.

Of course I was simply elated at how it had gone, and I hoped the people of America would be titillated to find out just what I had in store for the next week, so much so that they would pick up the phone or get on the internet and vote for me. They did, much to my relief.

I decided to do Walter T. Airdale next and have him yodel, something I thought people would enjoy, but the day after I had informed the producers of my decision, I was asked into a private room to discuss it. Georgie Hurford-Jones, an executive producer of the show, revealed that Simon Cowell had heard about my desire to yodel and really wanted to see me do Tony Bennett instead, adding that he wanted me to dress in a tuxedo with an open bow tie, a la the Rat Pack. Of course, the decision was mine, but I am smart enough to know that if Simon wants it, Simon gets it. I told Melinda that I thought of the show as a big game of Simon Says, and she laughed, agreeing with my decision to go with Simon's gut instinct.

Now I don't want you to think that I was getting preferential treatment. Simon had told all of the top twenty that he would help us in any way he could, and that he would give us advice but it was our decision to use it or not.

I asked if I could do two songs, Dean Martin's 'That's Amore' and Tony Bennett's 'I Left My Heart in San Francisco', and the producers said yes. They put together a cool sign that looked like a Vegas marquee, and I did the two songs.

After the performance the judges again complimented me, and this time it was Piers who mentioned the difficulty of what I was doing, and I was grateful again that he had reminded America of the hard work I had put into my act.

One of the defining moments of my entire life happened that night.

I have told you that I had decided not to create a persona for the show and to just bare my soul, resting my hopes on the idea that if America liked me, great, if not, at least I had been honest with them. For that reason I never tried to prepare myself for interviews and questions.

That night after I performed, Jerry Springer asked me what I hoped would come from all this. I answered honestly that I wanted to be a headliner in Vegas. Since I was a teenager I had dreamed of a long-distant date when I would come into Vegas and see myself on a billboard.

All I have ever wanted was to entertain people. My greatest frustration in life was that I had worked so hard to be the best I could and a very small percentage of the population knew who I was or what I did. Every show I did I had to prove to the audience that I wasn't your average ventriloquist, and I longed for people to want to come out and let me entertain them, starting every show knowing that everyone there expected a good and fun show, and I ached to deliver it to them. Fame and fortune would simply be a by-product of that desire, but the true end result I wanted was to just do the shows for appreciative audiences.

Is that what every entertainer really wants? I wonder. I have no idea of the answer to that, but it truly is why I love what I do. Don't get me wrong; when I was a kid I wanted to be famous for a lot of silly reasons. I remember thinking every time a girl rejected me when I was a teenager that they would one day regret it when I was famous, but I had long grown out of that phase, happy that life had taken the turns that it did and I had finally found my true dream partner in Melinda, and I hadn't had those thoughts since my teenage years.

I have to admit that I do enjoy getting recognized. I have heard that some people find it tiring, but I have yet to reach that point. I love it when people do a double-take and say, 'Aren't you…?'

Maybe I'm still a little immature, but it makes me smile.

I hope I never take for granted the people who come to my shows. I can't imagine that I will. I truly do like people.

Anyway, once I had said that I wanted to headline in Vegas the offers started pouring in! I got email after email, each with the promise that they held the key to my Vegas future, but one stood out from all the others. Melinda had meticulously researched every one of those who had promised me a life in Vegas, but she found very little to verify the promises they made, except for one who claimed he had never before solicited a client, but that he had seen me on *America's Got Talent* and was very impressed and could get me into Las Vegas as a headliner.

The company was TEI and the person was John McEntee. His website was truly legit and he had worked with huge stars including the Eagles, Aerosmith, Billy Joel, Ray Romano, Robin Williams, Jerry Seinfeld, Billy Crystal, Rod Stewart, George Burns, Dianna Ross, Stevie Wonder, and Lionel Richie. After a little investigating we found out that he had, indeed, worked with all of the acts I just mentioned and many more. With such an impressive array of talent he had been associated with I was amazed that he had contacted me!

He told me that he had never before been the one to contact an act, that they had always come to him, but that he had been compelled to work with me because of what he saw on the television show.

I called him and he invited me to his house for dinner to discuss the prospects of him managing me. Throughout my career I have had several 'managers', but none of them actually knew how to manage an act. It turned out that they were actually booking agents and they just charged an extra five percent for calling themselves manager.

I used my one day off from shooting AGT that week to visit John McEntee and his family. His house was unbelievable! It is hands-down the most beautiful home I had ever seen, and I realized that this guy was the real deal. We had a ball that night. He introduced me to his lovely wife Monica and after dinner John mentioned that he wished he could see more of my stuff. I excitedly told him that I had brought my puppets (something I have done for years: I always bring my puppets to parties in case someone wants a show. I LOVE to entertain and I always made sure if Melinda was with me she told the guests that I was a ventriloquist and would entertain if the partygoers asked) and would do a show if they wanted.

They loved the idea and I proceeded to pull out the puppets, one at a time, and entertain everyone. John and Monica were absolutely amazed at my range of musical styles and entertainment and both told me as I was leaving that although he had worked with some of the biggest stars in the world, they thought I was the best entertainer on the planet.

I called Melinda that night and told her I had been looking for a manager who felt this way about me, and that I really thought John McEntee could get me into Vegas. I agreed to let John represent me with a handshake that very night, and since then John has proven himself to be everything I had dreamed of in a manager: a tireless worker, promoter and friend, and it all happened because of that fateful night I said I wanted to be a headliner in Vegas on national television. Again, providence seemed to be taking a hand in my fate; the pieces of the puzzle that I had thought were missing in my life were falling into place at an amazing rate and I was loving every minute of it.

A very interesting thing happened to me about this time in the competition.

Several months earlier I'd had a friend of mine tell me a story that touched me to my very core. Apparently her friend had a son who became close to a little boy who was diagnosed with cancer. The two boys loved to play with toy horses and as the sick boy's health gradually declined he started to wonder out loud to his friend if there were horses in heaven. The two boys would discuss the prospect of heavenly equine creatures on a daily basis, until the sick child finally could no longer visit his friend.

After the boy's friend passed away his mother had a very difficult time trying to decide how to explain to her son that his friend had died, a difficult enough concept for an adult to accept, much less a child.

She finally sat her son down and told him simply that his friend had passed away, expecting questions and grief.

She was surprised, however, when her son happily said, 'Oh, I know. He came and visited me the night he died to tell me. Oh, and guess what? There *are* horses in heaven.'

As my friend told me the story my eyes filled with tears and I was overcome by emotion as I'm sure many of you are experiencing, just reading this.

My friend had heard some of my original songs (I am a songwriter as well as a ventriloquist). She said she had been searching for someone to write a song about that story and asked if I could take the task on myself.

I told her I would try, and began to think about it as often as I could.

I had not had any time to work on it at all since the show had begun, but one night after a particularly grueling day I awoke suddenly in the night with a song playing in my head. I had been dreaming about it, and it was still clear as it could be as I lay in bed thinking that we had an early morning and I had to get up in a couple of hours—and I couldn't be bothered by this right now.

A strong feeling kept prodding me to get up and write the song out. I protested as strongly as I could until I finally gave in to the urging and went over to my computer and began to write the song out.

Little Bobby playing with his six-year-old friend
Plastic horses gallop on imaginary wind
They play all day when Bobby asks
What he wants next year when he turns seven
With a sigh his friend replies
Are there horses in heaven?

Are there horses in heaven?
Can we ride them to the stars?
Will they take us up to Jesus and drop us off in His arms?
Will I know how to ride them?
Before I get to be seven I've just got to know
Are there horses in heaven?

The tears began to flow as I continued to write, knowing each line, remembering it from my recent dream.

After months and months of chemo
Bobby's friend is getting weak
He spends less and less time here
Now he can hardly speak
Bobby asks him what he wants
Next month when he turns seven
A tight hold on his little horse he says
Are there horses in heaven?
Are there horses in heaven?
Can we ride them to the stars?
Will they take us up to Jesus and drop us off in his arms?
Will I know how to ride them?
Before I get to be seven someone tell me please
Are there horses in heaven?

I was absolutely blinded as the tears flowed freely, overcome by the strong emotion of the words rushing through me and onto my keyboard. I knew something very special was happening, and I wept with grief mixed with joy as the last verse poured out of me into the laptop.

Bobby didn't see his friend after that day came
His mama couldn't find the words
Didn't know how to explain
She finally told little Bobby
Your friend never reached seven
Bobby said, 'I know mom, he told me.
Oh guess what?
There are horses in heaven!
There are horses in heaven!

We can ride them to the stars
Because they took him up to Jesus
And dropped him off in His arms!
And he knew how to ride them!
He never got to see seven
But now he knows:
There are horses in heaven!'

I saved the file and sat there and cried for a few minutes more, emotion welling up inside me and causing a lump in my throat so palpable I could hardly breathe. I determined that I would never keep any money from that song, that every penny it made would go to research of childhood diseases, and that was that.

How could I possibly make money myself on something that I had clearly had no input on?

Some may argue it was my subconscious mind that had manifested a desire to write a song about that story, and I'm sure that idea has merit, but I'm a simple guy and I like to believe that the song came from an outside source from me to make a difference in this world, and I'm sticking to that.

I immediately went to sleep after the song was finished and slept quite well for the hour and forty-five minutes left before I had to get ready for the next day.

I wanted something to commemorate the day, so as soon as I got to the studio I gathered all the other contestants together and I made a formal announcement that I had written a song the previous night that would be an enormous hit and that it would win lots of awards and be one of the top-selling songs of all time. I wasn't bragging, I really did just want the occasion to be marked by witnesses.

Everyone's reaction was exactly as I expected: laughter and teasing because many of the contestants were songwriters themselves and they were skeptical, but it didn't put a damper on my excitement. I knew it would happen and I still know it will happen.

The only question for you, the reader, is whether or not it has happened yet—or I am still waiting for it.

If you are reading this and 'Horses in Heaven' has been a huge hit all I can say is, I told you so. If not then just wait; it will be.

I can't believe I was given that song for no reason and I know it will make millions and millions of dollars of research money, to help alleviate the heartbreak of future generations of children and parents around the world. I'm not in a hurry. When it is supposed to happen, it will.

One thing I have learned in my life is that timetables are very often out of our control. I gave up on reaching many of my goals when I began to approach thirty-eight and decided that the world was never going to care about a forty-year-old ventriloquist, but I was proven so wrong on that count it makes my head spin.

I think one thing about life is that we must take control of what we can and leave the rest either to God or fate, whichever we decide to trust in.

I had to tell you that story since it was a huge event in my time at AGT and I think after people read about it in this book it will be fun for people to talk about it.

Won't it be cool when people read this and say, 'Wow! Terry called it! That song really was a big hit and he wrote about it before the fact!' At least it seems that way to me; but onward and upward with the story.

⁂

So I had impressed the judges once again, much to my relief and gratitude. I was constantly expecting the other shoe to drop and was always preparing for one of the judges to give an X, even if to just try and distract me, but thankfully it never happened. America agreed with the judges and voted me through to the next round: the final four!

My relief was complete. I had been watching the numbers on YouTube religiously and was extremely disappointed at how slowly they had grown. Cas, on the other hand, had enormous YouTube hits from the beginning and had already passed a million, while I was floundering around fifty thousand.

My cousin, Connie (who had changed her name to Lorraine since childhood but will always be Connie to me), kept emailing me the MSNBC online polls about who would win the competition. I had started out in the polls at the third from the bottom, and had slowly crept up the ladder until the final four competition when Cas and I were neck and neck, followed by Butterscotch, then Julienne Irwin. I think at that time I was eight percentage points behind Cas, a remarkable feat since I had started out a true longshot, at least in the MSNBC online poll.

From the moment I had started the show I had given myself absolutely no chance at all to win it. I was completely convinced that America simply would not be able to get past the initial gut reaction most people had towards ventriloquism: that it was for kids, and didn't belong in mainstream entertainment. I had hoped for years to change that perception, along with other vents like Jeff Dunham and Ronn Lucas.

I kept telling myself that if only I could make it to the next episode I would be happy. Just one more episode, that's all.

But now I was in the top four, and I decided that I had to give it my all. I didn't want to have to say for the rest of my life that I came in second or third or fourth on *America's Got Talent*; I wanted to say I had *won* it!

One thing you must know about me is that I am extremely competitive. I am a good loser and always have a gracious attitude toward the winner, should I find myself on the losing end of a competition whatever the occasion, but I don't like to lose. I will go to any amount of effort needed to win whatever it is I'm competing in. I've always been driven that way.

When I was fourteen, my cousin used to beat the pants off me in chess each time we played. I simply could not beat him. It drove me crazy, so I went to the library and checked out about ten books on chess strategy. I pored through them every waking moment, obsessing about every move from beginning to end, studying great chess games and how the masters had won them.

My cousin laughed and teased me, saying that no-one could learn chess from a book. The day finally arrived when I felt I was ready to compete and I challenged my cousin to a game.

I beat him soundly! I don't think he had ever been beaten in chess so badly, and he never played me again. I ended up entering a chess completion and took second place in Texas and went to a national competition—but threw my first game, because I realized that I was a teenager without my parents' watchful eye, so I ended up spending my time at the competition with some cute girls I had met. I was no dummy.

That competitive drive hit me hard during that final week of *America's Got Talent* and I decided I would play this sudden death game for all the marbles. I didn't think I had a shot, but it certainly wouldn't be because I hadn't given it my all.

As I had with chess, I obsessed over what I would do for the final episode.

Melinda and her mother, Shirley, had seen me sing Roy Orbison's song 'Crying' at the Fourth of July barbecue and were strongly urging me to do it. Debi had spoken about it a couple of times as well. I mentioned it to the producers of the show and their reaction surprised me.

'You can actually do an impression of Roy Orbison??' they asked incredulously.

I replied that, yes I could, and they agreed with Melinda, Shirley and Debi: it had to be 'Crying' by Roy Orbison.

The only trouble was that I had never actually done the song without moving my lips, so I had my work cut out for me.

Sometimes it is very easy to do an impression without moving my lips, as in the case of Garth Brooks' 'Friends in

Low Places', other times it can be extremely difficult and take a lot of time to get it down properly, like 'At Last' by Etta James.

I had no idea which case 'Crying' would fall into, but I submitted the song to the producers and it came back cleared. (When I say cleared I mean that in order for anyone to do a song on television you have to get permission from the writer. In some cases the writer refuses and the contestant has to choose a different song. Some of the contestants ran into a lot of trouble picking the songs they wanted, since the first few picks were refused. Luckily I never had that trouble and every one I asked to do was accepted. I'll tell a cool story about that in a little while so read on...)

I decided that Winston should be the one to sing the song since he had been so loved by people his first time out. I knew this because I received hundreds of emails from people all over telling Winston how much they loved him.

I was lying in bed late that night wondering how I would pull this off when an idea struck me. What if I put a wig and sunglasses on Winston so he would look like Roy Orbison? The very thought made me smile, and I called Melinda immediately and told her the idea.

She said, 'I think you may have just come up with a million-dollar idea!' I hoped she was right.

The next morning I told Elyse Foley my idea and she said exactly the same thing Melinda had said. Maybe I was onto something!

Now I had the song, and the idea of which character would sing it, so it was on to the hard work of learning to do the impression without moving my lips.

I called up Debi and asked her to order a new Winston, and outfit him with a little Beatles wig and sunglasses, and overnight him to me at the hotel.

I worked roughly ten hours a day to perfect the voice, spending every waking moment listening to Roy Orbison sing the song, trying to capture every little nuance in his voice, recreating it all through a tiny space in my mouth. I also carried Winston around with me and practiced every movement so that I wouldn't have to think about it during the actual performance.

Interviews, clothes fittings, rehearsal with the band, practice the song with Winston, hour after hour after hour. This was my last shot to win over the hearts of America and wow them enough to get them to their phones and computers to vote for me. I wasn't going to blow this opportunity.

I knew there would be plenty of time for fun later, but now I had to do this as well as I could.

Besides doing the song of my own choosing, the three judges had picked a song for all of the top four performers, to try to see if they could test our limits and get us to broaden our musical styles.

One of the luckiest moments of my life came when the judges decided that they would try to trip me up by choosing a country song for me. It just so happened that the song they chose was Garth Brooks' 'Friends in Low Places'!

There was absolutely no way they could have known that it happened to be the first impression I ever did as a ventriloquist, but there it was.

My producer Elyse was so excited when she told me, since she did know that I could do the song well, and I began to rehearse with Walter T. Airdale alongside Winston.

Debi had finished the new Winston with his wig and sunglasses and had FedExed him to the hotel, but when I went to the front desk to collect him they couldn't find him! I was in a panic. I told them how important he was to me and that I had a performance that could win me a million dollars riding on that little turtle and to please locate him.

After a worried hour they finally found him in a safe. Apparently someone wanted to make sure the box was somewhere secure, but neglected to inform anyone of its whereabouts. I can't tell you the relief I felt when I had him in my hands and was rehearsing the routine with Winston in his little costume. He looked as cute as I thought he would, and I knew America would fall in love with him.

The day of the final taping was at hand, and as I stood in the 'pools of light' (when the contestants who were left stood under spotlights on stage) waiting for my name to be called, I felt excitement welling up inside me.

I hadn't known conclusively if I was in the top four, but I felt confident after my Tony Bennett impression on the past week's show that America wanted to see what I had up my sleeve for the last week, and I was right. America was titillated enough to give me enough votes to put me in the top four!

I waited backstage with the other contestants and worked on my Roy Orbison voice right up until the moment they called me out in front of the cameras.

I heard my name and walked up to the microphone. Winston made a little joke and then started to sing. I could tell by the reaction of the audience and the look on the faces of the judges that it was going well.

Afterwards Winston and I received thunderous applause and a standing ovation. Even Piers stood up to cheer! I couldn't believe what I was seeing!

As the judges gave their assessment of my performance I felt the excitement welling up again.

All of them raved about it, and Piers said the only place I

would be crying was to the bank because I was going to win a million dollars! I was overflowing with happiness as I walked off the stage. I felt like a professional baseball player must feel after he has just hit a grandslam and won the World Series.

I still had no idea if I had won, but I did know that I had given it my all, and that was good enough for me. Later I performed 'Friends in Low Places' with Walter T. Airdale, and once again the judges were full of compliments, much to my delight.

After the show as my family and I gathered to eat dinner, I looked around at my loved ones, feeling so thankful to have such great people surrounding me. I knew I had given it my all and it was a great comfort to know that it was all finished and everything was now left in the hands of the American people.

I didn't think I would win it all, but I relished in the contentment of knowing I had done my best. There is something so satisfying about preparing as hard as you can for something and going out and doing the best job you can. I hope most of you know that joy, and if you don't, you really should. The hard work you put in is truly a reward in itself because you feel it inside yourself. I didn't need my dad to tell me I had done a good job that night. I didn't need anyone to; I felt it in the core of my being. I had prepared myself fully and I had delivered, period, and whatever America did with their votes, I could still feel good about that fact.

The following week dragged by as slowly as possible as we waited for the result show, which would take place live on national television.

On Friday the producers called me and told me that each of the top four contestants would be singing a song with a special guest star.

A few weeks earlier they'd had all of the contestants make a dream list of who they wanted to perform with if given the chance, and Kermit the Frog was the top of my list, along with Dick Van Dyke and Jerry Lewis, and many other great comedians who had influenced my life and career.

Friday afternoon I was called into a small room at the studio and saw cameras surrounding a telephone sitting on a table in the middle of the room. There was a couch next to the table and I was asked to sit on it and wait for a phone call from Melinda to tell me who I would be performing with. (She would come to the show's tapings but would fly back to Dallas every week so I could rehearse privately in our hotel room without interruption.) I had very little hope that she would tell me that it was Kermit since *America's Got Talent* airs on NBC and The Muppets are owned by ABC.

The cameras were rolling and the phone rang.

'Hello?' I said as I put the receiver up to my ear.

A familiar voice that was certainly *not* Melinda's said to me through the telephone receiver, 'Hello, is this Terry Fator?'

It was Kermit the Frog! I was stunned beyond belief.

I answered in the affirmative and Kermit exclaimed, 'This is Kermit the Frog and we are going to do a song together.'

Is it possible to explain absolute, pure, perfect joy with mere written words? All of the amazing emotions I had felt throughout the show's progress paled in comparison to talking to Kermit the Frog on the phone. My head was buzzing and he actually said to me that he was a big fan and that I was an amazing and very impressive performer. That's right, folks, KERMIT is a fan of mine! I think delirious is a good word to explain my emotion as he said that.

I don't remember much about the rest of the conversation, but he did tell me that we would be doing a song together and he was anxious to meet me. After I hung up I sat in stunned exhilaration for a few moments and tried to compose myself.

As I thought about what had just happened I realized that as I was talking to Kermit I had not been imagining a person holding a phone: in my head I had actually seen Kermit holding a phone up to his little frog ear (does he even have ears?) and that the conversation had been with Kermit, and not Steve Whitmeyer, the person who does his voice.

So now I knew who my special guest was, but what about the song we would sing?

Remember earlier I told you I had a cool story about song clearances? Well here it is:

The producers told me that the song they really wanted Kermit and me to sing was Carole King's 'You've Got A Friend', but that in spite of the fact it had been requested numerous times for shows like *America's Got Talent* and *American Idol* she had never allowed the song to be used.

America's Got Talent called her and asked for permission, expecting the same result as the other times they had asked, but when they told her that Terry Fator wanted to sing it she said 'Oh, I love him. Sure he can do it.'

When Elyse told me that story I couldn't believe my ears. I had toiled in absolute obscurity for decades and now Carole King was going to let me sing her song because she was a fan.

I called Melinda and told her, of course, and she was just as stunned to hear it as I was. Was I actually becoming a sort of celebrity? It kind of felt like I was, but I still wasn't sure.

The producers told me they wanted Johnny Vegas to sing the song in Tony Bennett's voice, but I told them I should do it like James Taylor. They asked if I did a James Taylor impression and I told them I could.

The truth is that I had no idea if I could or not, as I had never before done a James Taylor impression, but I knew that I would certainly give it my all for the finale.

I immediately went back to my hotel room and downloaded 'You've Got a Friend' off of iTunes and into my iPod and got to work. I worked late into the night and showed up for rehearsal the next morning ready to sing.

The producers were a little disappointed that my James Taylor impression was only passable, but I wasn't worried. I knew I still had two ten-hour days to perfect it.

As I had done with Roy Orbison's voice, I obsessed over every nuance of James Taylor's voice, listening to the song a hundred times or more, again spending every waking moment practicing, practicing, practicing. I even broke my rule about practicing alone. When I was at the studio I blocked everyone around me out of my mind and practiced no matter who was next to me.

I knew that the voting would be over, but I also knew that this would be my final chance to shine before millions of television viewers, and I wanted to make the most of it.

The next day the producers were amazed at my progress. They told me my James Taylor was much better. I knew I still had one more long day to get it just right.

Again I worked late into the night and got up early to rehearse even more, and by the time I got to the studio for our last rehearsal I was ready. The producers were stunned. They told me my James Taylor impression was perfect. They couldn't believe how much I had improved since two days earlier, and I just smiled and thanked them. They had no idea of the countless hours I had practiced.

Melinda had said from the beginning of the show that I made it all look too easy, and maybe that's true, but I think it's my job to make it look easy.

The audience's job is to simply enjoy the product of my hard work, not to be there when it's taking place or even think about it during the performance. If I don't make it look easy, then I feel I'm not doing my job right.

But I knew again that I had done my job and I was ready for my final appearance.

We pre-taped the song with Kermit the Frog since they had to tear out the judges' chairs and basically build a forest on the stage for the routine. I think it was the most fun thing I had ever done, singing with Kermit and meeting The Muppets. What an amazing thing to happen to me after all the years of preparation and hard work, but if I knew I had to do it all over again in order to get the opportunity to sing with Kermit, I'd do it!

I have already told you about the final show and the results of it, but if you've forgotten, feel free to go back to the first chapter and read it again. Go ahead. I'll wait.

Are you done? OK then, let's move on to what has happened since I was lying in my bed reminiscing about all of the events you have just read throughout this book.

Chapter 10

Who's the Dummy Now?

I think the thing that struck me first after life resumed was how very ordinary I felt.

Perhaps I had, in my deepest imagination, expected the 'celebrity fairy' to appear and hit me on the head with her wand and proclaim me a true celebrity; but alas, no such event happened.

We awoke (Melinda awoke, I got up after my all-night reverie) and dressed to do a remote interview for *The Today Show* on NBC, which was live in New York. We were still in LA.

Our car met us at the hotel, drove us to the studio and I did the interview, much to my excitement, but again, nothing about me had changed.

We spent the day doing interviews for the entertainment shows including *Access Hollywood* and *Inside Edition*, then returned to the hotel.

Melinda and I went over to the Universal City Walk to get something to eat, and we giggled a lot, quite delirious about the strange events of the night before, but the walk wasn't physically pleasant; the sun had somehow not been informed that I was supposed to be a celebrity now and had absolutely no care about how hot he made the day, so we broke out in a drenching sweat as we trudged over, the food cost and tasted the same, and doors didn't magically open for us because I had just won *America's Got Talent.*

During our little lunch together I had to excuse myself to use the rest room as I always do, so I guess I was not a celebrity yet or 'the change' had not occurred yet. Celebrities don't have to bother with hum-drum stuff like using the bathroom, do they? Surely they are above that common nonsense.

I mean, as much as we put them all on a pedestal so much higher than our lowly little selves and obsess over their every movement and decision, there must be something amazingly above our peasant way of life, and I secretly wondered when this change would come over me. Would it be quick, like taking off a band-aid, or would I slowly change like I was emerging out of a pod as in *Invasion of the Body Snatchers?*

I was anxious to find out. I had waited forty-two years to reach this pinnacle, and I didn't want to have to continue waiting to make the switch from regular guy to celebrity.

Did I need to call a celebrity hotline and give them my accomplishments, after which they would either stamp or deny my celebrity application, and I would at least know?

But none of it happened. Life went on exactly as it had before. Melinda and I even had our little daily snipes and snaps at each other. Winning a million dollars had done nothing to change that!

Our delirium lasted for several days until we were smacked down from the stratosphere of emotion to harsh reality so hard and fast it made our heads spin; I also lost an opportunity I had dreamed of for twenty-five years in the bargain.

Mel and I flew back to Dallas that Friday and my left knuckle began to hurt. Bad. My left knuckle (luckily not on

my puppet hand) turned bright red and was throbbing so
badly I couldn't sleep. It had started so fast and the pain was
so intense I really couldn't ignore it. I told Melinda about it
and she suggested I go to the hospital, but I pulled the macho-
man answer (I don't recommend it: it could have killed me!)
and said, 'No, Hon, I'll just go in tomorrow morning.'

The next day most of my hand was bright red and puffy
and the pain was more severe than anything I had ever
experienced. The hand was too swollen to bend in any
direction and I knew I was in trouble. I immediately called
my doctor and he agreed to see me right away. He examined
my hand and realized that I was in very dangerous territory,
so he called a friend of his who happened to be the best
hand doctor in the Dallas area.

The doctor took one look at my swollen, unusable hand
and called for the nurse to arrange for a hospital room. He
didn't say 'Stat!' much to my disappointment. He explained
to me that I had a very bad staph infection and that I needed
to get on some very strong antibiotics as soon as possible
to reverse the flow of the infection, which was racing at an
alarming rate toward my heart.

Apparently the stress and lack of sleep and working myself
close to collapse every night during the show had weakened
my immune system dramatically and a tiny pimple under
my watch had gotten infected in my hand and really wanted
to take me out like a hitman.

Within minutes I was in a hospital gown that tied up down
the back, on an uncomfortable bed with a tube attached to
my left arm to flush out the infection with the most potent
drugs of that type known to mankind.

To make matters worse the choice of television channels
was terrible and I had very little to watch during my lock-
up.

Melinda and Debi were concerned beyond words and spent several evenings worrying because my condition was terribly serious and could have gone in a tragic direction, literally in a heartbeat.

I received news that disheartened me, not because of my condition, but that the *David Letterman Show* wanted me to perform Monday night. I asked the doctor if I was up to it and he said that it would be impossible, since they had been infusing the antibiotics for twenty-four hours and seen no positive change. The infection wasn't spreading but it didn't seem to be going away either.

The doctor seemed worried, so when I asked him about my chances to fly to New York to fulfill a dream, he said that I would probably die on the trip if I took it.

OK, so this is a no-brainer. Death or Letterman. I certainly, in my wildest dreams, could never have thought I'd be facing that choice. Needless to say I chose to live another day and hoped I would get the opportunity to do his show again.

So the 'celebrity fairy' never arrived to whack me on the head and allow me to live above the common population.

Here I was, the winner of *America's Got Talent*, lying alone in a hospital room, waiting for the attendants to enter and put a new bottle of antibiotics into the tube in my arm and give me several painful shots of a blood-thinning agent into my stomach, to help the medicine go through my system quicker. Wake up, get shots, change over antibiotics, then try to sleep, try to watch TV, all the while more uncomfortable than I had ever been.

Monday night came and went and I watched the Terry-less David Letterman episode I was supposed to be on. I couldn't help but be a little depressed, but I turned off the TV and reflected on the strange turn of events during the last few days.

By now I knew for sure that no magic would suddenly turn me into a celebrity god and that life was going to continue on as it had for the first forty-two years of my life, only with different circumstances to enjoy and face.

I assessed my life up to this point (a good thing to do if you are in a life-threatening situation at the hospital!) and liked what I saw.

I had great friends that I would do absolutely anything for without any desire for compensation on their parts, and I knew that they felt the same way about Mel and me.

Many times throughout our lives together we had had to borrow money from more than one of them just to get by for a little while longer, and there was absolutely no strain in our relationship in spite of the fact that sometimes it took us several years to pay it back with interest. But our friends had never mentioned it, and opened their arms and houses to us as they always had, knowing that we were good for it when we got to the point where we could pay it back.

We had the exact same experience with our family. When we needed money desperately they had come through to help without judgment. Melinda's mom, Shirley, once gave us some money to help us out in a very difficult situation and I never heard it brought up again. I mentioned it to her a couple of years after the loan to tell her that we would pay it back when we could, but she replied that she trusted us implicitly and not to worry about it. When our credit cards were all paid down and we could get out of the crushing debt we had inherited from the band I had tried so hard to continue supporting (using Mel's and my credit card) she would then discuss with us a schedule, but not until we were ready for it. Our relationship with her didn't suffer one bit from it.

I will always be grateful for the amazing examples of our

friends and family about how to love above and beyond even fiscal troubles.

As I assessed my life I realized that I was a very happy individual. I had given up chasing the demon white rabbit who taunted me with his eternal elusiveness, promising that if only I caught him I would hear the words: 'I am so proud of you' from the one I had ached to hear them from for as long as I had thoughts.

Years earlier I had truly put the white rabbit to rest and had a nice imaginary rabbit stew that night. It was theoretically delicious, and more satisfying than anything I had ever consumed.

I no longer needed approval from my dad. I had proved him wrong on most accounts in his evaluation of my life, and one story completely destroyed his belief that God wouldn't call someone to a life of comedy.

I had done a show at a fair and was signing autographs and selling my merchandise afterwards. A lady waited patiently until I had finished and came up to me and warmly shook my hand. 'Do you see that boy over there?' she asked as she pointed to a row directly in front of the stage. I told her I did and tears began to stream down her face. 'That is my son. He was diagnosed with cancer six months ago and he hasn't so much as smiled during that entire time since that diagnosis. Tonight he laughed throughout your entire show. I don't know if I've ever seen him laugh so hard!' She thanked me for giving him the gift of laughter again and told me how much it meant for her to see him happy after so many long months of misery.

I went over to the youngster and gave him a copy of my video, a picture and CD and hugged him. His eyes were still twinkling with the joy he had experienced during my show that night.

I went to my hotel that night and I'm sorry to say that I promptly forgot about the episode until a few months later when once again I had finished a show and a lady came up to me afterwards and handed me a sealed envelope. Wordlessly she grasped my hand and smiled. I could see that her eyes were a little moist but she still said nothing and just walked away.

I put the envelope in my pocket and forgot all about it until I changed clothes that night and found the envelope the lady had given me.

I tore it open and began to read. I had to sit down as I read because the weight of what she had written me had such an impact on my emotions. My eyes brimmed with tears as I read. She thanked me for the gifts to her son several months earlier and went on to tell me that he had died two weeks after he had seen my show. But she also wrote that he had spent the entire two weeks watching my video over and over and laughing the whole time.

At his funeral they had set up a television and played my video next to his coffin so everyone could see what he had spend his last two weeks on earth doing, and she told me that she could never express her thanks to me for giving their entire family the gift of knowing her son had been so happy in his final moments on earth.

I don't think the impact would have been any greater if God Himself had appeared to me to tell me that my father couldn't have been more wrong in his opinion that God could not call someone to make people laugh. I think that family would disagree heartily, and I learned that day just how my silly little gifts can make a real difference.

I have never forgotten that moment and I will always be grateful to that stranger for sharing that with me. As I continued to evaluate my life I realized just how blessed I have been. I am surrounded by people I truly love and know I am a valuable part of their lives, as they are to mine. They have been honest about my abilities, and have reminded me constantly that I have worked very hard to become the best at what I have done and I should be confident and proud of my achievements for my own sake and not for the approval of others, especially my father.

All I could do was step on stage every time I did and give it my all. As long as I did that I could feel it provide the pride in my own psyche that I had reserved for my father my whole life, and without his input I found contentment.

~)

I got up out of that hospital bed when I wasn't getting the infusions and walked around the hospital with Winston the Turtle and went from room to room finding people who were suffering, some scared and alone, and entertained them.

Some were children, but most were not, but as soon as they saw me and Winston come into the room, child-like awe shone from their eyes and they forgot about whatever circumstances that had brought them to this dark place and they laughed.

One elderly lady looked like she had been in a car accident and her face was badly bruised. Her husband sat near with a grim look on his face, wondering if everything was going to be OK. I wish you could have seen the look on both of their faces as soon as Winston and I came into the room. She lit up like a light bulb, and a broad smile spread across her husband's face, and they laughed together as Winston started to sing like Kermit the Frog. I saw the husband's eyes get a little watery as he watched his wife laugh, for perhaps the first time in a while.

It was then I realized that all of the celebrity in the world doesn't amount to anything except to hopefully bring a little happiness into people's lives. I knew for sure now that my father had been dreadfully wrong about his assessment that God doesn't call people to be comedians. I don't think there is a preacher in the world who could have brought more healing to that little couple sitting in the dark hospital room that night.

That thought has been proven true more times than I can count as I continue to get emails and fan mail from people who tell me how watching me on *America's Got Talent* helped them get through chemotherapy, and the one thing which gave them strength to push forward in the darkest times was the drive to come and see my live show.

Some come up to me after they accomplish this goal (I try to always sign autographs and meet the audience after my shows. The only occasions I can't is if time won't permit) and I listen to them tell me about their struggles and how happy they are to have been able to come out. I smile and thank them for coming, realizing that every one of us has a great purpose in our lives, and I am truly thankful that I can help even in such a small way.

Soon after all this I went to Las Vegas to fulfill another dream (it's amazing how I have been able to fulfill just about every dream I have ever had because of that little NBC show!) of being on the Jerry Lewis Labor Day Telethon.

I didn't get to meet Jerry but I did get to perform on it and had a blast. What a hoot to actually be on the telethon I had watched since I was just a little kid!

I went to the airport to fly to my next gig and a lady came up to me to tell me that she was a big fan and had voted for me on *America's Got Talent*. She asked if she could get a picture, and of course I obliged.

She told me excitedly that she had flown to Vegas and spent the week there specifically during the Labor Day Telethon because she had wanted to meet a celebrity.

'I can't believe it!' she exclaimed. 'I finally got to meet a celebrity!'

'Really?' I replied? 'Who did you get to meet?'

She looked a little surprised, and then she laughed. 'You!'

I had to laugh. I apologized, telling her that I was still new to all of this.

I got to go on the *Ellen DeGeneres Show*, and when Ellen told me she was a big fan I just couldn't believe it. Ellen a fan of mine? Is this real? How is it possible that people I have been fans of for years are now fans of mine? I still have a hard time wrapping my brain around that.

Life continued to whiz by at breakneck speed, and my dreams kept coming true one by one.

When I was fifteen years old I decided that I wanted to be the best ventriloquist in the world and that I would like to one day headline in Las Vegas. I would close my eyes and imagine seeing myself on the marquee. There it was! Terry Fator. It seemed so real, but as I became an adult and continued to struggle in obscurity the dream got less and less tangible. Would it ever happen?

When I turned thirty-eight I began to visualize it even more intently. Every time I went to Las Vegas I would step off the plane and I would close my eyes when I got to the place where the banners were advertising the headliners and I'd try to see myself up there with them all. I felt that I had the talent; someone who could put me there just had to see it too. Then I had my Vegas fiasco in February of 2007 where the producers told me I wasn't Vegas material. Luckily Melinda thought they were full of it and told me so.

But one man, John McEntee, knew better than those three producers. He had seen me on *America's Got Talent* and when he heard me say that I wanted to headline Vegas he contacted me and told me he could get me into Vegas.

I signed with him as my manager and he came through. He had already booked me as a headliner at the Las Vegas Hilton in their main showroom three weeks before I won *America's Got Talent*, somehow convincing them to take a shot at a complete unknown, something unheard of in Vegas.

It turned out that the gamble paid off. As soon as the tickets for my first Las Vegas headlining show went on sale, before any advertising had been done, the show sold out in four days.

America wanted to see my live show and the Las Vegas Hilton was stunned! They had never had a show sell out before they had even advertised it, so they asked me if I would do a second one. That sold out in a week. So now I had two sold-out shows at the Las Vegas Hilton, the very place Elvis Presley appeared whenever he played Vegas.

I even got to use Elvis' old dressing room!

I couldn't wait until the day of the show, and John McEntee proved to be far more than just a manager.

He wanted to help me completely revamp my act and get it Vegas-ready. I was ecstatic!

Melinda had always said that if only we could find someone to believe in my talent I could have the best act in the world. John believed it as well and put his money where his mouth was. He invested much of his own money (to be paid back when I got the check for doing the actual show) and helped to bring in all sorts of cool stuff, even helping me come up with a new character. We worked non-stop to get ready for my Vegas debut.

The biggest hurdle to all of this was that Melinda and I had pretty much hocked our whole future on *America's Got Talent*.

Originally we had been told that it would tape in the spring, so I didn't book anything during that time.

It turned out that the show was to be taped during the summer, so I had to cancel pretty much the whole summer's worth of my paying gigs to do *America's Got Talent*.

Don't get me wrong; there was no choice. I knew that AGT was my big chance so I knew I had to do it, but watching our bank account drain at an alarming rate and having absolutely nothing going into it was a desperate feeling.

After I won, I knew it would be several weeks before the check actually came in so Mel and I discussed how in the world we were going to pay our bills and keep from going under, until either the check came or I could start doing the higher-paying gigs, as a result of winning.

John McEntee came to the rescue without our even having to ask. Mel and I were discussing who to borrow money from when John called me up and said, 'Terry, I'm not sure how your finances are at this point, but if you need anything call my office and I'll wire money into your bank account. I need you to be concentrating on your show right now and the last thing I want you to do is worry about money. You can pay it back when you get the AGT check.'

Problem solved. Did I get lucky by finding an awesome manager or what?

I had decided that no matter what the show was, if I had booked it before winning *America's Got Talent*, I was going to do it. Some of them were under terrible circumstances and the money wasn't great—but I didn't care. The last thing I was going to do was shaft the folks who had booked me before I had my good fortune. I fulfilled every contract, much to the surprise of all the fairs. I was surprised how everyone expected me to cancel. I was told that it is not very often people keep to the agreements and do the shows for the original amount settled upon, once they hit it big.

That's a shame. If we don't have our word, we don't have much in my opinion.

All in all it was a lot of fun and most of the fairs I played had record attendance on the nights I was there to do the free shows.

I was asked once in an interview what the biggest change is since I became a celebrity (it is still hard for me to think of myself as a celebrity!) and I replied that before, when I was performing at a fair if I asked for a fruit tray they replied, 'Get your own darn fruit tray!' Now when I ask for a fruit tray they say, 'Is twenty-eight varieties of fruit enough?'

It's the craziest thing. Before, if I asked for bottled water they laughed at me and pointed to the nearest vending booth, now I get four cases just for asking. Go figure.

But I think the best change is that I hired a road manager. His name is Foley and he is the greatest thing to happen to me since John McEntee.

Before Foley I had to do everything for myself. I set up my puppets, did sound checks, got my own luggage, made sure the hotel was in order, everything. Then I hired Foley and now the only thing I have to worry about is my act. Can you just imagine how awesome it is to have someone take care of all the little annoyances that had become commonplace in your life? Believe me, it's great, and I know that my show has really benefited in amazing ways since I have very little of the strain and stress I used to, and not only do I benefit, but you, the fan and paying customer, benefits as well, since when you see my show, you can know that I am able to give you all of myself because of all the hard work Foley does behind the scenes. So if you ever see him after one of my shows make sure to thank him for all his dedication!

Anyway, I made it through all of the old bookings and had a wonderful time at it (again, thanks to Foley). I got to meet some great people, and once again I was overwhelmed at the humanity of it all. So many stories, so many people, and I was (and still am) grateful to be a part of it all.

The night arrived for my Vegas debut. I was downstairs in my dressing room (Elvis' old dressing room, don't forget!) surrounded by my new band and many of my friends and family. I sat on the couch and watched everyone buzzing around and I smiled as I thought about how much fun my family and friends were having. The food warmers kept a buffet of tasty things hot, and everyone was eating and drinking and talking excitedly about how surreal this was.

I had never actually thought about how all of this would affect my friends and family. When I was striving for success, all I thought about was Melinda and Debi, but I was delighted to see how proud everyone was as they got to be part of the backstage scene of a major headliner, and that headliner was me! I think delirious is way too tame a word but it'll have to do.

A few minutes before the show, everyone left to get to their seats and I was alone in the dressing room with Melinda. She asked if I was nervous. I told her truthfully that I wasn't, I was just excited. This is where I belonged and I knew it. I felt so comfortable and at home here.

John McEntee had arranged for me to have a live seven-piece band headed by an amazing musician, Scotty Alexander, who had played for several years with Wayne Newton. We had spent the last several days rehearsing and getting ready for the big night, and I was anxiously waiting stepping out on the stage.

I made my way to the stage area and took a deep breath.

The music started and the voice-over said, "Terry Fator!"

I walked on stage and the audience leapt to their feet. The applause was deafening and went on for what seemed like minutes. I couldn't help but stand there, drinking it all in, smiling from ear to ear. I was here! I was on stage at a major casino headlining to a packed house and the audience was standing up for me, anticipating a great show. I had done it! This is all I had ever wanted. I had longed for so many years to not have to spend several minutes of every show proving that I could entertain the crowd. I wanted people to come out to see my hard work, not be wandering around a fair and accidentally stumble onto me. That night I got it all. I think there were seven or eight standing ovations and I've never been so happy to be out on a stage doing what I love to do so much!

My first two nights at the Hilton were the hardest tickets in town to get. I was told that even other casino presidents had tried to get tickets and couldn't because it was a capacity crowd, standing-room only.

I have never had more fun in my whole life than I did those two nights, but even now after headlining many more times (the Las Vegas Hilton was so impressed with the show and the ticket sales they signed me up to headline three shows a month during 2008) I still get that amazing feeling every time I step out on that Vegas stage. I also still get all giggly every time I fly into Vegas and see that huge billboard on the way to the hotel. Can you blame me?

I had waited forty-two years to headline, and each show in Vegas is truly a dream come true. I hope I never take it for granted.

When it was all over and my friends and family were in my hotel room snacking and reliving the night's exhilaration, we just reflected on the amazing journey I had been on, especially in the last few months.

But it was far from over. Things continued to come together in ways I couldn't have possibly imagined.

I was asked to perform for a private dinner for Nancy Reagan and accepted readily, but here's the clincher: as they introduced me to her she smiled brightly and said, 'Oh I know who you are! I watched you and voted for you. I'm a huge fan!'

Now, how do you respond to that? An icon like Nancy Reagan knows who the heck I am? How does one even process that? I mean, no-one knew or cared anything about me as an entertainer until I was in my forties, but now Nancy Reagan is a fan!

Of course, I thanked her and did the show, after which she told me how much she enjoyed it. I saw her laughing very hard at a few of my routines and at one point I think she laughed so hard she had to wipe tears away. It was fun.

The next day I got to go to a luncheon to meet President Bush. One thing I can say about President Bush is that he is truly one of the warmest people I have ever met. He made Mel and me feel like we were important, congratulating me on my success and chatting with Melinda about moving to Texas.

'We can be neighbors!' Melinda said cheerily.

With a twinkle in his eye, the President said, 'I don't think you want to have me as a neighbor!'

He shook our hands warmly, congratulated me again and moved on to the next person waiting to meet him.

I don't know if he remembers the meeting but I was struck by how genuine he seemed and I felt very important that day, and Melinda did too.

I hope I do the same for those I meet. I truly do love

people and I enjoy meeting them, and I hope I always convey that.

I continued to meet celebrities, and I found that in spite of the fact that the media makes celebrities out to be something bigger than life, they are just as you and I are.

I think the big thing about celebrity is how you arrive. I was lucky to have truly found happiness and contentment in my life before all of this, so when it happened, I was and am able to enjoy it all.

I think if someone is hoping for celebrity to fix insecurities they will be severely disappointed. It doesn't matter how many people tell you how great you are, if you don't already know your worth it won't matter a hill of beans to your psyche. Very little actually changes about who we are, it's really only our circumstances that change, and I think maybe it could be a shock for someone who thinks celebrity and money will suddenly make all their problems go away.

Just as I had needed to have my father's approval for so many years, and it didn't matter how good I got or how many people told me how good I was, I still ached for that one thing. It was only when I found my own worth that I was able to let it all go and just enjoy what I had been given.

My father had told me constantly that I wasn't very good, and that I was just clever at fooling people into thinking I was good, and I lived my life thinking I was a fraud and that my while life was a house of cards that would come crashing down on me once everyone figured out that I wasn't really as talented as they thought.

But letting go of it all and just getting comfortable with how God had made me, and being happy with the friends and family I had truly set me free.

I no longer needed my father's approval, I had my own approval now, and that was all I cared about. I could do the best job possible for my own pride and satisfaction. I would walk off every stage knowing that I had put in the best effort I could, and every new routine I wrote and performed was the best I had to offer, and if people liked it, great, if not, I knew I had given them my best. That attitude was what got me through *America's Got Talent*, and still keeps me going every single day.

See how the ADD-addled brain works? One minute I'm telling you about meeting President Bush and the next I'm psychoanalyzing the entertainment industry. Believe me; you don't want to have to live with this brain of mine!

So let's get back to the narrative.

I continued to do more and more shows, having a wonderful time entertaining people all over the country at community theaters and corporate events and getting to meet them after the shows. It was so much fun because I no longer had to drum up crowds. Also, when I had done corporate performances before AGT I always had to deal with people saying stuff like, 'They booked a ventriloquist for this? What were they thinking?' But now the audiences were excited with the anticipation of seeing Emma sing 'At Last' and Winston singing 'Crying'. I was in heaven.

One day my cell phone rang. It was John McEntee and he told me to sit down.

'Are you ready for this?' he asked.

'Yeah, what is it?' I replied hesitantly.

'Oprah's people called. They want you on the show!'

I shot out of my seat and whooped for joy. I had been asking about doing Oprah's show since I had won AGT.

I asked what the show was about. John told me that Simon Cowell was to be the guest and Oprah wanted him to discuss the top two acts he had ever seen during his career, and he had named me as one of the top two along with

Leona Lewis, a pop star who had recently been discovered (by Simon, of course!).

So now I was to be on the *Oprah Winfrey Show* as one of the top two entertainers on the planet, according to Simon Cowell. Does life get any more surreal than that? I mean, could this really be happening to me?

A few years earlier I had gone to Vegas and had imagined myself on the billboard like I described to you a little while ago, and as I looked up and saw Danny Gans staring back at me from the billboard I thought, *I guess that kind of stuff doesn't happen to the Terry Fators of the world, they only happen to people like Danny Gans.*

I could not have been more wrong because now here was Terry Fator about to perform on *Oprah*!

OK, I admit it. I have something a little silly to tell you, but I think you should know. When I was about thirty-five I started to carry a Sharpie magic marker in my pocket all the time. I told myself that one day I'd be famous and that people would want my autograph, so I wanted to be prepared.

Even when I had lost faith in the dream, I never quit carrying the pen. I couldn't let go of the wisp of the dream, so I never took the pen out of my pocket. It sat in there unused for years, and now I've had to replace it several times since I actually do sign a lot of autographs, but it started with a dream, hard work, and an encouraging family.

And I did the *Oprah Winfrey Show*. She shouted 'Wow!' six or seven times after the performance, the pinnacle of which was my newest character Julius (the one John McEntee helped me create) singing Marvin Gaye's 'Let's Get It On' right to Oprah herself. Simon beamed with pride at having had the show that discovered my abilities, and thanked me after the Oprah appearance for helping to make *America's Got Talent* a big success.

Are you kidding me? Simon Cowell thanked me? I asked Melinda to pinch me when it was all over. Had that just really happened or had I had a nervous breakdown and was locked up in an asylum somewhere having delusions of grandeur?

I want to admit something to you now that I haven't told anyone yet, not even Melinda. She'll have to read about it just like you. I can't wait to have the conversation where she says, 'You've got to be kidding me! You made me read it like everybody else in the world? You couldn't have just told me about it?'

But that's OK. At least I'll know if she's ever read the book. If she never mentions it to me I'll know that she hasn't read it! Hee hee hee.

Anyway, here it is: As Oprah was announcing that Simon Cowell had called me one of the top two entertainers on the planet I actually thought to myself, *I hope somewhere my father is sitting watching television and sees this. I think Simon's opinion has a little more weight than my dad.*

OK, I know it's petty but I couldn't help myself. I felt such a sense of pride at that moment to have Simon say what he did on national television, and even though I had given up the need to hear it from my father, I also think maybe a part of me got even more than I had ever hoped for in that moment. I still don't ever want or need to hear from my dad ever again. Some people are toxic and my father is one of those. He literally leaves a swath of heartbreak and devastation in his wake like a class-five tornado and I have no desire to allow him near enough to ever bring despair to me or my family again, but I have to admit in my deepest thoughts that I hope he knows about it all. Even so, I'm sure he still thinks he's right and I am just good at fooling everyone into thinking I'm talented and one day I'll be revealed as a fraud. (As I'm writing this I can't help but smile.)

So I got to be on Oprah and it was a ball. Melinda and I spent the next day or two in delirium over it all, wandering around Chicago like in a dream, laughing about how different our lives were now from a year ago.

I continued to do tons of shows all over the country, flying to Vegas once a month to perform at the Hilton. Life was more fun than even my dreams could have envisioned, if not exhausting.

Playing at the Hilton had been such a wonderful experience and I developed wonderful friendships with many of the employees: Rick White, Ken Ciancimino, Ira Sternberg, Eric D' Richards, Tony Tauber, Julie Burke, Jinny Largent, Julie Crozier, and, of course, the security guy C.J. (who looks a lot like Julius the puppet. In fact, his family now says that the J in C.J. stands for Julius!), plus many more.

C.J. remembers the suit I wore the first time I ever played the Hilton. It was the one with the velvet jacket I had on when I sang *What a Wonderful World* with Winston. I was so proud of that velvet jacket and I loved wearing it, but now several months later I have been able to have many custom suits made (I love it, by the way. I've never been a suit guy, but I am now) and I wear a different suit every night I perform now. I wandered around wide-eyed those first couple of shows like a deer in the headlights. C.J. says, 'It is so much fun to have watched you come in here the first time with only one suit and now you have all these beautiful suits and you take such command of the stage.' I think he has enjoyed all of it almost as much as I have.

I had accomplished just about every dream I had ever had since I was a child. I had proven to myself that with a dream and hard work anything was possible. Up until now I had no idea what was around the corner, something so huge I couldn't have even dreamed that big.

About a decade earlier I had been begging God to let me win the lottery, explaining all of the great things I would do with the money if I could only win it. I would buy a ticket every chance I got, again begging to win.

One day a tiny voice said in the back of my head, *'You have everything you need to win your own lottery. Just make use of it.'* I have no idea if the voice was from someone outside of me in a spiritual sense or if my own brain was just telling me something I knew deep inside and needed to be brought out into my conscious mind, but it made a huge difference in my life. I quit buying lottery tickets and started working on my talents. I dedicated myself to being the best I could at every show and I was also determined to make sure every character I created was the most creative I could make it and I would do my job to the absolute best of my ability and left it at that.

And now here I thought, all of my dreams had come true, but I was wrong about that. Life had more to offer and I was about to really be blown away.

I told you earlier that I had dreamed of being on *David Letterman* since 1983 and I still had not been able to do it. I felt that the magnitude of being on *Oprah* and *Ellen* had made up for it, and to a great degree it had.

Unfortunately for me I have always been very anal about specifics when it comes to my career. I am one of the most laidback people in the world about life in general, but I want my shows to be absolutely perfect in every way. Mistakes don't really bother me since I truly believe the audience is coming out to have a good time and as long as I am delivering that, even when I make a small mistake, I always turn it into a joke for the audience to be part of.

When I say the show has to be perfect, I simply mean that I expect myself to give every ounce of my energy and devotion to every audience that comes along every single night, without exception.

So this part of me kept nagging me about the David Letterman show. I knew I had been able to do amazing things, but I had dreamed of being on Letterman for so long I couldn't let it go.

I had been so incredibly busy that I had had to turn him down in February and it absolutely broke my heart, but again, I had contracted shows and they always came first.

Then my publicist, Cheryl, called. 'Terry, I've got great news. Letterman's people called. They want you on the show in May and we have a date set!'

I almost cried with happiness. After twenty-five years of dreaming and working toward this dream, I was finally going to do it. When I had first started dreaming about it, David Letterman was on the very late time slot and since then he had taken over the legendary Ed Sullivan Theater, so not only would I get to be on his show, but I was going to be performing at the Ed Sullivan Theater as well.

As I waited for the day to arrive I got more and more excited.

Did you think that doing the Letterman show was the thing that was even far beyond my wildest dreams? If so, you couldn't be more wrong. I was about to get news that absolutely blew me away. I'm only telling you the story like this because this is how it happened chronologically, and I want you to see it just like I did.

So anyway, I had just found out I was going to be on Letterman and I was chomping at the bit to get to New York and do it, but it was still several weeks away. I don't like waiting. I was one of those kids who got all hyper as Christmas was approaching (what am I saying? I still do that) and I was starting to get really annoying to Melinda.

'Getting all worked up isn't going to make the weeks go by faster,' she would say, but I just got more jittery and excited.

Meanwhile, things are going on in Vegas that are about to set in motion things I couldn't even have dreamed up a few years earlier.

Melinda read the stunning news that Danny Gans was leaving the Mirage for another casino showroom. She wondered out loud if I might be able to replace him.

Yeah, right. *Me* have my own theater at the legendary Mirage Casino in Las Vegas, the place Siegfried and Roy had started and became legendary entertainers. Oh, yeah, I'm sure that would happen.

My assumption had been that I would get an extension of my Hilton contract and continue to play there once a month for a few more years.

I have to admit that after more than twenty years of traveling around performing I had started to ache for a home life. It is something I've never had and the idea of getting up from my own bed every day, doing a show and going home to my own bed to sleep every night was certainly a tempting thought, but this was a pipe dream. Headline at the Mirage. Have my own theater at the Mirage. That just doesn't happen to guys like me, right?

I was in a hotel room when my cell phone rang and it was John McEntee again.

'Are you sitting down?'

I sat down and assured him I was.

'Put Melinda on a conference call; I need you both to hear this.'

I did as I was told and Melinda and I sat and waited in our respective places to hear what John had to say.

'I've just finished a meeting with the executives at the

Mirage Casino in Las Vegas. You are their new headliner. You'll be starting February 14, 2008 in the Terry Fator Theatre. You will also have your own merchandise store right in the Mirage. Congratulations, you've just signed one on the biggest deals in Vegas history!'

He told me the amount of money I would be making and Melinda and I just sat stunned, unable to say anything.

I was too stunned to yell, whoop, holler, anything. Who could have possibly foreseen this? That a few years earlier I had focused on a dream with all of my heart, body, and soul, and now it had manifested itself in ways I couldn't have imagined.

After John got off the phone Melinda and I laughed and cried, and I said, 'Well, I guess I just won the lottery!'— except this was so much better, knowing that the blood, sweat, sacrifice, and tears of myself and my family had brought it about. I felt that I had earned this, and my heart welled up with gratitude and pride. I thanked God for all He had given me throughout my life and I promised never to lose that gratitude.

I can never even begin to explain how it feels to have every dream you have ever even considered, and more, suddenly granted to you within the span of a year. I hope one day you can come out to the Mirage to see my show and feel the excitement because I won't be losing it any time soon! And then afterwards I will get to go to my own bed in my own home and get a good night's sleep. Ahhhh, that's the life!

After Mel and I talked for a while, I called up all my friends and family and glibly told them that I had signed a multi-million dollar deal to headline at the Mirage. It hadn't actually hit me yet.

I was talking about it like it was just the next part of my career. That was on the Thursday night.

I woke up Sunday morning and my brain exploded. 'HOLY COW! I'M HEADLINING AT THE MIRAGE!' were my exact thoughts.

I lay in bed absolutely stunned as the reality of it sunk into my core.

I called Foley that morning and he said, 'You sound different. Did it just hit you?'

I laughed and said, 'Yeah, it did.'

I called Melinda and she said, 'You sound different. Did it just hit you?'

Again I laughed and repeated my last phrase.

It was a good thing I was alone because I think Melinda would have killed me that day. I bounced all over the hotel room the whole day. I'm surprised no-one had to scrape me off the ceiling with a putty knife.

Now I have to tell you this story. I am doing this for every single one of us who has had that *Pretty Woman* moment in our lives.

You know which scene I mean: the one where we get that snooty look from a sales person because they think we are too low-class to be in their store.

Well, I had one of those moments the day after the reality of the situation hit me. I was still buzzing seriously, but I had become at least grounded enough to float just a couple of inches off the ground instead of four feet.

John McEntee had told me that I needed to start dressing nice since I was now a representative of the Mirage and I agreed. Unfortunately I like to dress casual and slouchy (read: comfortable) like most of the rest of us and I had sent all of my suits to the cleaners that morning, so I had nothing to wear but my trusty blue jeans and a pullover shirt. I was comfortable, but not high class by any stretch of the imagination.

I decided that I needed to get a new pair of sunglasses because the ones I had were old, cheap, and scratched.

I walked around for a while, found a little up-scale sunglasses shop and entered.

The sales lady looked down her nose at me as if to say, 'Why are you wasting my time?' She frowned and said, 'Can I help you?'

I smiled, 'I need some new sunglasses.'

'You do realize that these are very exclusive and expensive sunglasses, don't you?' she retorted, a look of sourness exuding from her. Her nose was pointed so far up in the air I knew if the fire alarms went off she would drown instantly.

I ignored her and looked at the man standing next to her and said, 'Can you show me some sunglasses, please?'

'Certainly sir,' he cheerfully responded.

I know he probably thought it was all a waste of time but at least he was courteous and very nice. We went through more than a few pairs of sunglasses as the snooty lady prowled around the perimeters of the shop, making her disapproval known that the salesman was wasting so much time with me.

As we were looking at a very cool pair, the lady strode up to me and asked, 'Where did you get the sunglasses you wear now?'

'Wal-Mart,' I replied truthfully

Without a word, she turned and walked away.

OK, it's on. I am not leaving here without a pair of sunglasses! I thought to myself.

I know, I know, it's petty, but I was so irritated. I knew that even if they were expensive, Melinda would understand once I told her the story of what had happened. I always try to inform her when I buy stuff that costs more than a little, but this time I simply was not going to leave that store without buying something. We looked at a few more pairs and I finally settled on one I really liked. They looked great and fitted even better.

'Now normally I wouldn't be able to get these, but I have just recently signed a multi-million dollar deal to headline at the Mirage so I'll take these,' I announced, loud enough for Miss Sour-Puss to hear.

The man who had helped me and another young sales lady both started talking animatedly. 'You're that guy!' they exclaimed. 'We just read about you in the paper this morning.'

The look of shocked amazement on snooty lady's face was priceless. She stood, stunned, unable to speak, and gawked. The guy rang up the sunglasses ($1700!) and I went on my way.

I have to admit that I never even knew that the world contained a pair of $1700 sunglasses, and now I owned a pair, but all I could think of was how the guy who had helped me had just made a big commission. I laughed as I put my new sunglasses that cost as much as a used car on my head. I felt light as I walked down the street. I could hear Julia Roberts in my head holding up her bags of goodies, saying to her own snooty sales ladies, 'Big mistake. Huge!'

I told Melinda the story later that night and, before I even got to the end of it, she cried, 'Big mistake! Huge!' and we had a good laugh about it.

So for all of you out there who will never get that opportunity, I proudly salute you and say: that one was for all of us normal folks out there!

OK, so I had to indulge a little, but it sure was fun.

It turned out that having to put off Letterman for so long was a blessing because we got to announce the Mirage deal to a national audience that Thursday.

I did the show that week and had about as much fun as is possible.

The night before the show Mel and I were watching TCM and they were playing a night of Frank Sinatra movies and Melinda told me that it was the tenth anniversary of Frank Sinatra's death. It hit me with a sudden revelation that that very night had been extremely significant in our lives.

Exactly ten years earlier Melinda and I were up watching the news when they announced that Frank had passed away. It was then that Melinda had mentioned she wanted us to try to get some independence from the band I was in, and she wanted to get a job so we could get our own apartment instead of living with a bunch of musicians struggling to make it.

I agreed and we had spent the night combing the want-ads. Melinda found a job that looked perfect and we stayed up the rest of the night watching Frank Sinatra montages on all the news channels.

At 9am Melinda had called and asked for an interview. They wanted to see her that very morning, and without any sleep we drove the one-and-a-half hour trip to the Hillside Veterinary Clinic so Melinda could interview for the job. She got it and it led to our first taste of real independence as a married couple. Exactly ten years later to the night I was one day away from being on David Letterman and had also just become the new headliner at the Mirage. Wow!

As had happened to me countless times during the past year, my head was buzzing with elation as I stood backstage, met Paul Schaeffer, went on stage and fulfilled a dream I had had since my college days in 1983, making David Letterman laugh and cheer for me. I can't even tell you how wonderful it felt to have this one under my belt, but I am never one to stop, once I accomplish something I have dreamed of.

Just as all of my wildest dreams (and some even beyond my wildest) have manifested themselves and come true, as I bask in the warmth and satisfaction of the moment I am still thinking of new goals I want to accomplish, so I know that I must continue to work toward those new experiences.

I'll give you an example.

Just after Melinda and I started dating seriously we were at a little bar performing in San Angelo, Texas.

Melinda ran sound for the band and we lived out of hotel rooms, but we also had a little motor home so we could freshen up at the club and not have to go all the way back to the room during our breaks.

Mel and I were outside the front of the club during one of these breaks and the most beautiful, sweetest little cat either of us had ever seen came right up to us and plopped on the ground on her back in front of us.

Since both of us have always been cat people (we love dogs but cats are our favorite pet) we were instantly in love with this cute-as-a-button feline.

We took her into the motor home and played with her for hours during each of our breaks, and Melinda took her back to the hotel room to live with her during the rest of our stay in San Angelo, or at least until we could find the cat's owner.

She was so sweet we just knew she must belong to someone—so we dedicated ourselves to finding who that might be, but to no avail. No-one anywhere in the area had any idea who she might have belonged to so we adopted her. She belonged to Melinda and me since we were a couple, but I don't think anyone had any delusions who the new cat really bonded with. Melinda and this new kitten became inseparable. We named her Lamu (after an island off the coast of Africa)

I originally got the name from a song by Christian contemporary singer, Michael W. Smith, in which he sang about this tiny paradise island, but I always thought Lamu would make a great name for a cat and I was right.

Lamu was, in our opinion, the greatest cat that ever lived, and anyone who ever met her agreed. She was a special little cat. There was something about her that was just amazing, and she lived with Mel and me for more than sixteen years before she died of cancer.

She had been our little companion through some of the roughest patches in our lives together, and had always been such a comfort and joy to come home to no matter how difficult the situations became. I always wondered if my lack of desire to have kids didn't stem from my father's constant reminders to his offspring what a burden we had been to him, but I think it is because I chose my career over having children.

Losing Lamu was one of the most difficult times of our lives. I know that losing a pet can only pale in comparison to the pain of losing a child, but I also know that Melinda and I had formed a bond with Lamu and the ache in our hearts was as real as anything, and to see her go was emotionally devastating.

As Melinda and I wept over the limp body of our little angel who had loved us wholeheartedly for almost two decades, I told Melinda to get ready because we were going out. She protested, but I insisted. Melinda got ready and we carefully wrapped little Lamu's furry body in a nice towel and went to Melinda's clinic to leave the remains with them, so they could put her in an urn.

We got to the clinic and I told Melinda to go upstairs to where they kept the abandoned and lost kitties and to pick one out; we were taking it home.

Again she protested but I said I was not leaving that clinic without a cat and if I had to, I would pick one out myself and bring it home.

Through her tears Melinda whispered, 'Well, there is this one sweet little boy cat named Sammy...'

Turns out Sammy was having a hard time finding an owner so he went home with us that night. I was absolutely resolute that Melinda would never live in a house without a cat in it. It is as much a part of her as her soul, and I knew that she would waste away without a companion to share her life, since I spent much of my time on the road.

I promise that there is a point to this story that actually has to do with the fact that I am always looking for new goals and dreams to pursue, and believe me when I tell you I am getting to the point, but before I could get to it I had to fill you in.

So anyway, we get back to our place with this new cat and he is checking out his new home, sniffing here and there and trying to figure out just what the heck is going on. Melinda was following him around like a shadow, laughing at every little cute thing he did, and I smiled to hear her giggles, knowing that through the ache in her heart she was sowing the seeds of a whole new bond of love.

I sat out on our patio and drank a glass of wine slowly, gazing at the moon as she leisurely made her way from one end of the sky to the next.

I thought about Lamu and how great she had been. Something about her made her really special. Even strangers who met her sensed something really cool about her, and I am not exaggerating about that.

Melinda and I would brag about her to friends who had their own cats, and they would roll their eyes and talk about how great their own cats were, but then when they met

Lamu they would all say, 'Boy, you were right. That is the greatest cat ever!'

It was so intangible that you really had to meet her in person to get it.

So I am sitting out on my patio sipping wine and thinking about Lamu and smiling as I remembered her little habits, and I had a sudden thought.

She was such a great cat, I thought to myself, *She would have made a perfect pet even for Jesus!* Then I qualified myself, *If Jesus had owned a cat, of course!*

I was amused at the thought, but I really did believe it, also.

It is said that Jesus was perfect (and many believe it to be so), and Lamu was so good she would have made a great animal companion for him.

I went inside to hear Melinda laughing about something Sammy had just done (much to my delight) and I told Melinda my silly little thought.

It made her smile. 'That is such a nice idea.' She thought about it for a moment with her eyes closed, a contented smile spreading across her face.

When her eyes opened she said, 'You should write a book about that.'

A book? Was she joking? I have massive ADD, I could never write a book!

But the idea never went away, and I have started writing a series for children about the life of Jesus, as told through the eyes of his cat, Lamu.

My point is that in spite of the fact that all of my dreams have come true even beyond my wildest expectations, I have new goals to accomplish. Once I have settled into my new life at the Mirage I will begin to work toward getting the Lamu series finished. Who knows? By the time you read this they may be done and you can go get them right away. I will tell you that the stories I have come up with are fun to read and will enthrall you and your family.

But the dreams keep coming. I have heard that without a vision, people perish. I will never live my life without a vision.

When I was twelve, we had a guest speaker at school who told us that no matter how much we prayed and asked God to open the door of opportunity for us, if we weren't set to go through it when it opened we may lose it forever. I made a decision then that I would always be prepared— and if anyone with me wasn't ready, I would not lose my opportunity because of them. What I mean by this is a matter of work. TEXAS the band never wanted to work so I had no trouble leaving them behind to pursue my own goals because I wanted to work my butt off to get there.

I feel that God will do His part for us but He won't do it all. He will see to it that the opportunities arise but it is entirely up to us to determine if we are prepared. I had no idea as an eager twelve-year-old that I would have to toil for the next thirty years before that door opened and I could walk through it.

I have told people I've worked with in the past many times that if they aren't ready for the next step and it arrives, I will go on without them, and I have had to keep my promise to them every time it happened. I have never once been dishonest or sneaky about it, but several times I have moved from one level to the next, and if those I was working with have not been preparing themselves for that next level, they were left behind to continue at the level they were stuck at.

At one point as my success was really sky-rocketing I had one of my agents (I had only worked with him a couple of years so it wasn't a long-term relationship) grumble because

I had signed with a guy who was getting me a much higher paycheck for each show. This particular agent complained because he said he could have gotten me that kind of money, it would have just taken him four or five more years.

I looked at him, dumbstruck. 'Are you kidding me?' I exclaimed. 'I have been working at this for twenty years! I'm not waiting another five if I can get to my next goal now, just because you aren't ready yet!'

The interesting thing was that he had done the exact same thing to my previous agent, but he couldn't understand why it would happen to him.

I had always been honest and above board with all of my agents. I made it very clear to them that I wanted to make as much money as I could, and get as much work as I could, and if I ever found someone who was better than they were I would go with them.

I honestly wasn't trying to be mean about it, I just wanted them to work hard with me to accomplish the goals I had made for myself, and if they did that, we all benefited! I also felt that by having such a relationship with them would motivate them to work harder to ensure they are ready for the next level of success, just as I was doing.

None of them were prepared for my winning *America's Got Talent* except John McEntee, who, like me, had worked his entire life for the opportunity to be ready when someone like me came along, someone who had the talent and the drive to hopefully set the entertainment world on fire.

We have had so much fun coming up with new ideas. He had, like me, worked his way up from nothing, hocking his whole life to buy a nice car and a nice suit so he could take clients out and impress them. He had worked tirelessly to be the best at everything he put his mind to, and also to always be upfront and honest, and never burn bridges. John

McEntee and I are truly a match made in heaven. We are always writing new material and talking on the phone about the next routine, and the ones who benefit are the people who come out to my shows because I will always have fresh new stuff for them to enjoy.

I tried so hard to help some of my other agents along because I really wanted them to be able to be a part of my new success, but after several months of begging them to figure out how to work at this new level I had to leave them behind. They just weren't ready when the door of opportunity opened, and I was not going to let them keep me from walking through it! I was always very generous to those who took part in my success, however. I made sure they were compensated fairly for their role in my career. It's only right, after all.

If I had known how long it would take, I wonder if I would have had the patience to continue? I have no idea. I only know that I never thought about the timeline. I only focused on making sure I was ready. I made certain that every time I set foot on stage I gave it my all, whether I was performing for a room full of first-graders or one twelve-year-old kid at a fair in Texas.

I could never let myself get sloppy because that one guy who would see my potential and take me to that next level might be right out there amongst the audience of eighteen, as I churned out yet another performance on a stage that was open to the hot sun at that fair in Montana.

I never gave into the temptation to schlock out a show and just rest on my laurels. I gave absolutely everything I had to give to every audience I performed for, and because of that I got into the habit of doing my job right.

When I got on *America's Got Talent*, so many people commented on how natural I looked, how I took such command of the stage and owned it from the moment I walked out.

What they didn't see was the thousands and thousands of shows I had endured to hone my craft and teach myself that confidence, to allow me to do my job and make it look effortless. Time after time after time I kept going when there was no end in sight, and I never surrendered to the nagging doubts that crowded my brain as I lay exhausted and lonely in a dumpy hotel room, phone pressed up to my ear talking to Melinda about the day. I could feel the dirt and sand from the three shows at the dusty fair crunch between my teeth, as well as the salt and grime all over my face, and I would debate whether or not I had the energy to take a quick shower before I collapsed into sleep so I could feel refreshed enough to do it all over again tomorrow. Mel and I would talk and dream while I ate a cold hamburger because I hadn't had time to eat during the day.

For more than twenty years I had trudged through that life, seeing many worthy souls come and go without fulfilling the dream.

But because of my family and friends and the determination that I was going to get what I dreamed of no matter how difficult my circumstances, I pressed on.

I had won *America's Got Talent*, been on Oprah, Letterman, Ellen, met the President, had Simon Cowell call me one of the top two entertainers on the planet, sold out numerous shows at the Las Vegas Hilton and had now been named the major headliner on the Strip in Las Vegas at the Mirage (for an unbelievable amount of money) where legends are made, all in the span of less than a year, after my seemingly endless struggles.

So after it is all said and done, the hard part is over, the work is just beginning, and the dreams have all come true.

What happened to the boy who suddenly got everything he ever wanted?

He lived happily ever after.

Maybe next time it'll be you.